A Christian Critique
of Socialism

by
Donald A. Hay
Fellow and Tutor in Economics, Jesus College, Oxford

GROVE BOOKS

BRAMCOTE   NOTTS.

CONTENTS

Copyright Donald Hay 1982

THE COVER PICTURE

is shared by this and its companion booklet no. 5a, *A Christian Critique of Capitalism*, and is by Peter Ashton

First Impression May 1982

ISSN 0305 4241

ISBN 0 907536 22 0

1. INTRODUCTION

This essay is intended as a companion to *A Christian Critique of Capitalism* published earlier in the Grove Ethics Series. It has been delayed in the writing, and apologies are due to those many friends who urged its production earlier. However it is possible that publication now is more apt. Recent events on the British political scene, especially the divisions within the Labour party, and the emergence of the Social Democratic Party, have focussed attention on varieties of socialism. We have resisted the temptation to enter the contemporary political scene with a Christian critique. So there is no analysis here of the politics advocated by current political leaders, nor of the philosophies outlined in the recent writings of Shirley Williams, David Owen, and Tony Benn. However it is hoped that the reading of this essay will help the thoughtful reader to make his own Christian assessment of the types of socialism at present on offer.

The essay distinguishes three types of socialism, though the differences between them are not in practice so clearly defined. The first is communism, characterized by a powerful state which directs the economy by means of planning. The second is a neo-marxist socialism, which has updated the Marxist analysis of capitalism, and seeks to introduce socialism by a quiet revolution in which the state takes over giant companies and co-ordinates their activities by a limited planning mechanism, and by strict control of the financial sector of the economy. The third is the social democratic tradition (note the spelling—small 's' and small 'd'—to make clear that the Social Democrats are not necessarily implied). This tradition rejects much of Marx's analysis of capitalism, and proposes a socialism which involves detailed regulation of a capitalist economy and society, without the abandonment of capitalist firms and enterprises as the basic productive units. These three types of socialism, and their programmes, are described in some detail in the next two sections of this essay.

It may surprise some readers that so much of the analysis concerns economics. They might ask whether the proper emphasis ought not to be a broader vision of the nature of man in society. Thus the comparison between capitalism and socialism might be made in terms of individualist versus collectivist philosophies. However the fundamental point which all types of socialism have inherited from Marx is that the organization of production is the key to understanding all relationships in society, not least the question of the locus of power, and how that power is exercised. Hence the focus of socialist programmes *is* economics, and unless we understand the economics we will not understand the socialist system and ideals. However the economics cannot be divorced from ethical issues, as if it were merely a technical matter. On the contrary, all sorts of ethical issues arise concerning the state, property, planning, freedom, work, and equality. So we have chosen to tackle these one at a time, providing the ethical tools for the evaluation of each variety of socialism. Naturally the degree to which these issues arise will vary between one variety and another. A further advantage of this approach is that it will enable the reader to make his own evaluation of other socialist programmes which are not dealt with specifically in this essay, e.g. the Chinese model, and the application of social models in Third World situations. The First World bias of the essay can only be excused by the observation that it is already twice as long as the companion essay on capitalism!

An important theme which is not treated in what follows is the contribution of Christian theology to the development of socialist thought. Christian socialist movements in the nineteenth century owed much to work of F. D. Maurice, an influence which continued in the work of R. H. Tawney. British socialists such as R. H. Crossman and Tony Benn have acknowledged an intellectual debt to Richard Niebuhr's work *Moral Man and Immoral Society.* No doubt other links exist, which are worthy of full consideration in some other essay than this.

The essay is deliberately left without conclusion, for three reasons. First, the whole piece has been written consciously as an *essay*: it is a first attempt to get to grips with the ethical issues of socialism. It is not intended as a complete work. Criticism and comment will be greatly appreciated, so that errors, omissions, and obscurities, can be rectified in later writings. Second, it is hoped that the reader will be able to use the ethical principles outlined in the essay to make his own assessment of the socialist programmes currently proposed, and the variants which will no doubt emerge in the coming years. Third, there is a serious difficulty in applying the arguments which is not dealt with in the essay. It is that most applications require a consideration of the 'trade-offs' between one objective and another. For example, how far are we prepared to sacrifice efficiency for more equality? Or economic freedom for ethically more acceptable methods of organizing production? In the utilitarian framework of economics the problem is resolved by attaching utility 'weights' to various objectives to enable the trade-offs to be quantified. But this is merely a smokescreen, as the question of arriving at the appropriate weights is not solved. It is not a question to which Christian moral philosophy has given much thought. It merits much greater attention.

2. SOCIALIST ANALYSIS AND SOCIALIST IDEALS

There are many varieties of socialism, but each and every kind starts its agenda at the same point, a fundamental and rooted dislike of capitalism and its effects. This is the source of its moral purpose and energy, and it is towards the solution or alleviation of the problems of capitalism that socialist programmes are directed. So it is necessary to outline briefly the socialist critique of capitalism before directing our attention to the socialist society or programme which is the subject of this paper.

(a) The Marxist Critique of Capitalism

The Marxist analysis of capitalist development is conveniently outlined in *The Communist Manifesto,*[1] though the full subtlety of Marx's system did not emerge until the publication of *Capital.*[2] According to Marx, the industrial revolution destroyed the simple hierarchies of feudal societies, and replaced them with a two-class system. The bourgeoisie are the owners of capital, the proletariat are the workers employed by them. The emergence of the bourgeoisie is based on the technological revolution in manufacturing industry and the development of free trade. Competition ensures that only the strong and efficient survive in the market place. Large scale and mechanization (with consequent division of labour) are the means to achieve efficiency. So success is related to the accumulation and concentration of capital. However the system has two fundamental flaws. The first is that competition between capitalists tends to drive down the rate of profit, thus removing the capitalist incentive to accumulation. This long-run trend towards decline in the profit rate is accentuated in crises of overproduction, when the intensity of competition between capitalists leads to the closing down of productive plant and to losses for some of the bourgeoisie. But, despite this difficulty, because they retain control of the means of production, the bourgeoisie are able to maintain their grip on society, and, in particular, political control. The second flaw in the system is its ultimate dependence on the proletariat. The capitalist system can only develop insofar as it develops a working class. The workers can only survive by selling their labour as a commodity to the capitalists. In production they become appendages to the machine. Because of the nature of the productive process, they become alienated from their work. Competition between the workers for employment keeps the wage at a subsistence level, and hence the surplus from their labour accrues to the bourgeoisie. The workforce is 'disciplined' by periodic crises in the capitalist system which leave many of them unemployed for a while. This only serves to increase their dependence on the bourgeoisie for their continued existence. Eventually however, the very process of capitalist production, in bringing the proletariat together for production and giving them a common lot, provides also the means for combinations of workers to form trade unions. Initially they will operate locally, seeking to raise

---

[1] K. Marx, F. Engels *The Communist Manifesto* (1848, English translation in D. McLelland (ed.) *K. Marx: Selected Writings* (O.U.P. Oxford, 1977)).

[2] K. Marx, *Capital* (Three Volumes. English translation by B. Fowkes (Penguin, 1976)).

wages, combat closures of factories, and improve working conditions. But later they will seek to strengthen themselves by forming alliances with trade unions in other areas. Despite this, they will not be able to improve conditions materially, because of the long-run decline in the profitability of manufacturing which will lead the bourgeoisie to resist vigorously the attempts of the trade unions to raise wages. The proletariat will then come to realize that improvement can only come by the destruction of the system itself. The capitalists must be dispossessed of the means of production, since their interests block any reform. So the organization of the proletariat turns itself into a revolutionary movement:

> 'The Communists disdain to conceal their views and aims. They openly declare that their ends can only be attained by the forcible overthrow of all existing social conditions. Let the ruling classes tremble at a Communistic revolution. The proletarians have nothing to lose but their chains. They have a world to win.'

The Marxist analysis is a mixture of descriptive and moral elements. Whatever the merits of the historical analysis and its associated historicism, the moral fervour still commands attention. Four elements can be distinguished.

First, the actual social and economic conditions of the working classes in nineteenth century Britain, as described in *Capital,* chapters 10 and 15, were simply appalling.

Second, the alienation of man from his labour, so that he becomes a wage-slave and his work merely another commodity, is evidently evil.

Third, the fact that the system, while keeping the workers in abject poverty, also generates a surplus for the capitalists to maintain their lifestyle is open to objection on the grounds of inequality.

Fourth, the control by the bourgeoisie of the means of production enables them to maintain a grip on society and to make decisions in their own interests without reference to the interests of the vast mass of the people, the proletariat. Because of the nature of the capitalist system, there is an inherent tendency to crisis. But in a crisis the bourgeoisie arrange for the costs to fall most heavily on the working class, in terms of lower wages, unemployment etc. So the lot of the working class is made worse by continual uncertainty about their future, a future which is entirely in the hands of the bourgeoisie who make all decisions in their own (class) interest.

(b) The Neo-Marxist Critique of Capitalism

The Marxist analysis still attracts a substantial following among socialists, though the context of the analysis has been updated[1] to

---

[1] The modification of the economic analysis is seen clearly in the work of Holland, Baran and Sweezy and to a lesser extent Sawyer and Aaronovitch. (See: S. Holland *The Socialist Challenge* (Quartet Books, London, 1975); P. Baran, S. Sweezy. *Monopoly Capital* (Monthly Review Press, New York, 1966); M. Sawyer, S. Aaronvitch *Big Business* (Macmillan, New York, 1975)).

meet the different conditions of the twentieth century. The centrepiece of the analysis is the development of giant manufacturing firms, particularly those with a multinational flavour. These are seen as the logical conclusion of the capitalist process of accumulation. Confronted with the threat to profit posed by competition, the large firm has sought to achieve a monopoly and to control its market. If the market is worldwide, then only a multinational can achieve this result. By this means the capitalist sector has held off the long run decline in profits foreseen by Marx, and has also made itself less vulnerable to 'local' capitalist crises. However the crises of world capitalism are still an important difficulty for the system. The relationship of capitalism to the bourgeoisie has also changed subtly. No longer is there a direct link between the ownership and the control of capital. The diffusion of shareholding has enabled a new managerial class to assume control. The managerial élite are distinguished by their identification as individuals with the success of the particular companies which they control. The company rewards them with power, prestige, salary, and all manner of non-pecuniary benefits. Their interests are particularly served by the continuing existence of growth of their company. It has served their interests to make an alliance with the remaining bourgeois class of property-owners, shareholders, etc., and they have aspired to adopt the lifestyle of that class in terms of consumption, emphasis on private education, and political attitudes. Particularly they have been successful in obtaining a continuing policy of aid to the capitalist sector in terms of grants and subsidies from general taxation. These have helped to keep the profit rate up, and have enabled the system to weather the occasional capitalist crisis.

The position of the workers has changed in one vital respect. Their material lot has improved very greatly, for a number of reasons. First, the extension of monopoly and the obtaining of subsidies from the state, has enabled the firms to concede trade union demands for rising wages, since there has not been so much pressure on profits. Second, the development of a welfare state paid for from general taxation, and not from capitalist surpluses, has reduced the militancy of the proletariat. But the other essential features outlined by Marx have not changed. The worker is still alienated from his work: indeed the pace of technological advance has made this more critical. A new breed of worker has emerged who accepts passively an utterly dehumanizing job for the sake of a large wage to spend in his leisure time. Third, though there may have been some reduction in income inequality, the managerial/bourgeois class maintains a high standard of living on the basis of the surplus created by the workers. Class interests and identification are as strong as ever. Finally, the power of big business has largely replaced the power of the bourgeoisie, but the worker is still at the mercy of the decisions taken by the managers of big business. Even democratically elected socialist governments have been able to do little to weaken their power over the workers. For example, a multinational corporation can use its threat to transfer its operations to another country to fend off an intervention by the government on behalf of workers.

(c) The Social Democratic Analysis of Capitalism

Even less of the Marxist analysis survives in social democratic writings.[1] Writing in the late 1940s and early 1950s, the analysis was particularly directed to the situation in Britain. Crosland argued that Britain could no longer be classed as a capitalist country. First, government intervention in the economy had become pervasive during the war. Governments were much more prepared to control the economy generally, using Keynesian demand management to maintain full employment. Second, the owner-manager class was disappearing, and being replaced by professional management. Shareholder control was weak. Third, as a consequence of the previous point, the ownership of the means of production was becoming irrelevant to its control. The alienation of workers derived more from the technological basis of modern methods of production. Fourth, the simple Marxist analysis of class conflict between the bourgeoisie (capitalists) and the proletariat (workers) no longer applied. The new conflict was between workers and management, and it was a conflict where significant transfer of power to workers had occurred. Keynesian full employment policies had blunted the capitalist weapon of unemployment as a means of disciplining the workers. The nature of modern production methods made strikes extremely costly for the management, so that industrial action had become a powerful instrument in the hands of the trade unions. Fifth, the unequal distribution of wealth and income is no longer a strictly class matter: wealth is not concentrated in the hands of an identifiable capitalist 'class'.

The conclusion is that the social democratic analysis has rejected much of the Marxist analysis. But the moral motivation for social reform remains. Crossman[2] writes that social progress is measured by 'the degree of equality and respect for individual personality expressed in the distribution of power and in the institutions of law and property within the state. This standard is what we mean by the socialist ideal'. Jenkins[3] spells this out: 'where there is no egalitarianism, there is no socialism'. For him, a classless society is the goal: 'one in which men will be separated from each other less sharply by variations in wealth and origin, than by differences in character'. With this general ideal, particular areas for action are identified. There is an awareness that in any market economy there are likely to be significant minorities who are materially disadvantaged. The relief of poverty is, therefore an important goal. Even when material poverty is absent, capitalism will generate significant disparities in income and wealth. Crosland[4] argues that this will lead to social discontent based on envy. He regards envy as a basic human response, which must enter any realistic social analysis. it is important because it manifests itself in collective

---

[1] See, for instance: E. F. M. Durbin *The Politics of Democratic Socialism* (London, 1940); C. A. R. Crosland *The Future of Socialism* (Jonathan Cape, London, 1956); R. H. S. Crossman 'Towards a Philosophy of Socialism' in *New Fabian Essays* (edited by Crossman) (second edition, London, 1970).
[2] Crossman *op. cit.*, p.10.
[3] R. Jenkins, 'Equality' in Crossman *op. cit.*, p.69.
[4] Crosland *op. cit.*, Chapter 9.

discontent, which feeds on itself and generates social tensions. The analysis is reminiscent of Hirsch's analysis[1] of the failure of material progress to bring happiness. The lot of the workers has improved in absolute terms, but they are no nearer to obtaining the coveted 'positional goods'[2] which by definition are available only to the few. The achievement of equality of opportunity is an important socialist ideal. But this is not enough in itself, if the resultant distribution of income and wealth is markedly unequal. Equality of opportunity is hindered by the privileged access to education and to positions of economic power, which is fostered by inherited wealth, and by birth into the wealthy classes.

Democratic socialism is also motivated by the rejection of competition as a social organizing device, and by the espousing of an ideal of co-operation. There are two elements in the co-operative ideal. First, personal motives should involve the idea of working for the common good rather than for oneself. Second, relations at work should be guided by co-operation rather than antagonism between workers, managers, and owners.

Finally, there is an awareness of the dangers of the concentration of power into the hands of the few, as the result of technological and organizational progress. Crossman[3] quotes approvingly the view of Reinhold Niebuhr[4] that human institutions have an unceasing proclivity to act immorally. So a constant watch must be kept on their performance with a view to preventing the worst excesses. One consequence is that the large companies in the private sector must be properly scrutinized in their activities and made responsible to social objectives. Further, large institutions, whether in the public or the private sector, must not become the preserves of small managerial or civil service élites. Managerial positions should be filled on the basis of merit, and the managers themselves should be subject to some wider democratic control. In particular, decisions affecting employment should not be taken solely with regard to the interests of the institution.

---

[1] F. Hirsch *Social Limits to Growth* (Routledge and Kegan Paul, for the Twentieth Century Fund, London, 1977).

[2] Positional goods. By definition there can be only one Prime Minister, one chairman of ICI, a limited number of generals, and rather few professors. Not every aspirant to one of these positions will be able to attain it, however well he seeks to qualify himself. Similarly, the 'exclusive' tourist resort is no longer exclusive after it has been discovered by a large number of tourists. Keeping *ahead* of the Joneses is a tiring and frustrating activity.

[3] Crossman *op. cit.,* p.12.

[4] R. Niebuhr *Moral Man and Immoral Society* (UK edition, SCM Press, London, 1963).

3. SOCIALIST PROGRAMMES

Corresponding to the social analyses described above there is a variety of socialist programmes. The purpose of this section is to describe these in broad outline. At the end we will identify those issues that require scrutiny from a Christian ethical viewpoint.

(a) The Communist Programme

Marx gave little detailed attention in his writings to the kind of society which would follow the proletarian revolution. The main sources are *The Communist Manifesto*[1] and the *Critique of the Gotha Programme.*[2] His lack of precision is related to his theory of history. The new society would *arise* out of the capitalist society by means of the revolution. So its form would be historically conditioned. He had no socialist utopian ideal, and tended to criticize those who had. In the *Critique of the Gotha Programme* he saw two stages in the development of the society after the revolution. In the first stage the proletariat achieves power, and extends to all the workers the principles of the bourgeois society. The producers become the state and take control of the instruments of production. This stage was given the title of 'Socialism' by Lenin.

Marx outlined in *The Communist Manifesto* ten regulations which would be characteristic of this stage:
1. Abolition of property in land and application of all rents of land to public purposes.
2. A heavy progressive or graduated income tax.
3. Abolition of all right of inheritance.
4. Confiscation of the property of all emigrants and rebels.
5. Centralization of credit in the hands of the State, by means of a national bank with state capital and a national monopoly.
6. Centralization of the means of communication and transport in the hands of the State.
7. Extension of factories and means of production owned by the State: the bringing into cultivation of wastelands, and the improvement of the soil generally in accordance with a common plan.
8. Equal liability of all to labour. Establishment of industrial armies especially for agriculture.
9. Combination of agriculture with manufacturing industries: gradual abolition of the distinction between town and country, by a more equitable distribution of the population over the country.
10. Free education for all children in public schools. Abolition of children's factory labour in its present form. Combination of education with industrial production etc.

A number of features are noted by Avineri.[3] Nationalization of industry is not included as an immediate measure. The private sector will wither

---

[1] K. Marx, F. Engels, *The Communist Manifesto* (1848, English translation in D. McLellan (ed.) *Karl Marx: Selected Writings* (O.U.P., Oxford, 1977)).
[2] K. Marx, *Critique of the Gotha Programme* (English Translation in D. McLellan *op. cit.*)
[3] S. Avineri, *The Social and Political Thought of Karl Marx* (C.U.P., Cambridge, 1968) Chapter 8.

away in the socialist state without direct expropriation. The abolition of private property is not advocated. Marx himself criticized the advocacy of 'crude communism' by idealist socialists. Simply reducing everyone to the same level would make each person a worker for *State* capital. It would do nothing to liberate men from the productive relations of capitalism. Rather, in Marx's scheme the proletariat uses the power of the state for their own ends. The programme itself is not particularly revolutionary.

But for Marx this was merely a first step. He distinguished a 'higher phase of communist society', which would succeed it, and which was entitled 'communism' by Lenin. This phase is even less defined in his writings. However it is to be marked by a new consciousness in man, a new attitude to work, a new basis for production, and a new form of state. Man's relation to things will be creative rather than hedonistic. Work is not the evil which it appears in capitalism. It is part of being human. The creation of needs will simultaneously create the means to ensure their satisfaction. Work constantly unfolds the potentialities of the individual. Each person contributes in accordance with his abilities. The precise form that productive activities will take in this phase is not spelt out. It is significant that Marx relies on illustrations from agrarian societies, where rigid differentiation or social division of labour is less apparent. Nor is the role of planning clear, except in so far as co-operation between workers is necessary to achieve social objectives in the absence of a market mechanism. The State itself is to 'wither away', but not in the sense (due to Engels) of its total disappearance. Rather it is to cease to operate as a social institution divorced from the totality of economic life: universal suffrage will ensure that it remains responsive to the needs of the people and not separated from them. Finally, we should note that the 'communist' phase can only be reached when there is abundance in terms of material production. We might note that Lenin predicted that the Soviet Union would move into this second phase in about 1980!

Whatever Marx might have thought would follow the revolution, the reality in Eastern Europe has been somewhat different. The basic pattern was developed by Lenin, and propagated by Russia in its East European satellites. There are variants, of course, particularly outside the Soviet bloc.

There are four basic elements[1] involved:[2]
1. All power in economic matters is concentrated in the Communist party which seeks to promote the interests of the working classes. The party provides for continuity in economic policy, and makes the basic value-judgments about the long term objectives of

---

[1] It is worth noting at this point that these four elements do not include direct controls on the individual in terms of direction of labour or determination of private expenditure patterns, nor is the right to hold a certain amount of 'private property' abolished.

[2] J. Wilczynski *The Economics of Socialism* (Third edition, G. Allen and Unwin, London, 1977).

society. It should be noted that its influence extends beyond economic matters, and is pervasive in all aspects of life.

2. The means of production are socially owned, especially natural resources and capital equipment. This applies to agriculture, industry, banking, finance, distribution and foreign trade. Small private or individual sectors may survive, but their activities are severely curtailed.

3. Market processes are replaced by, or supplemented by, economic planning. The macro-economic objectives are determined by the Communist Party. The economic planners operate to those objectives.

4. The system seeks a socially equitable distribution of the real national income, where income is defined as the individual's share in real goods and services. There is no money income from property: all earned money incomes are based on the quantity and quality of work that is done. Private consumption is supplemented by a well developed system of collective goods, provided by the State.

In principle, this system is designed to meet the objections to capitalism identified by Marx. The absence of a capitalist class, and the control of the State by the proletariat, remove the major source of class conflict. Since all capital is owned by the State on behalf of the proletariat the alienation of workers is partly removed. There is no longer a surplus that is appropriated by the bourgeoisie: in principle at least, the surplus is used by State to further the interests of the workers. Such alienation as remains relates to the technology used in production, and possible antagonisms between a managerial class and the workers. Planning is intended to remove the uncertainties of the market economy, particularly avoiding the crises of overproduction. Thus long run security in income and employment is supposedly assured. Finally, the control of the distribution of income, together with abolition of property income and the plentiful provision of public goods, removes the threat of extreme poverty, and could prevent persistent disparities in income levels. Whether the system can actually deliver these social objectives, and at what cost in other areas, is something which we must discuss further below.

An important alternative to the Soviet model, though still claiming to be 'socialist', is the Yugoslav system of worker-managed enterprises. The centrepiece of the system is the labour-managed firm. Any group of workers may set up an enterprise, subject to no more legal restriction than applies to a public company in a capitalist economy. The enterprise is owned by the workers. Most firms of any size operate by means of a workers' council which has the responsibility of recruiting managers and other key personel, and which approves an annual plan of operation for the enterprise. This plan approves in advance the rules for remuneration of the workers in the enterprise, the principle being that each worker is remunerated according to his work. The level of remuneration actually paid then depends on the success or otherwise of the enterprise. The plan also specifies the distribution of the firms' incomes to other objects—notably reserves, acquisition of new capital assets, and social or welfare expenditure, e.g. housing or sports facilities. Within the guidelines laid down by the workers' council, management has in practice considerable freedom of action.

The role of the State and the central Communist Party is much truncated under this system. 'Planning' is reduced to determination of the overall allocations to capital investment, social and personal consumption. The supply of finance to enterprises is controlled by State banks, which in principle can be used to guide investment decisions. The provision of social goods—especially education, health, and social insurance—is important, and is paid for by taxation on both enterprise and personal incomes. Taken together with the collective goods provided by the enterprises themselves, this gives a ratio of social consumption to personal consumption which is much higher than is usual in a capitalist economy.

(b) The Neo-Marxist Socialist Programme

Neo-Marxist analysis has also generated a socialist programme.[1] The power base for the execution of such a programme is a democratically elected socialist party with its origins in the trade union movement. We should note the point made by Avineri[2], that even Marx himself suggested that attainment of universal suffrage in Britain could obviate the need for a revolution. So the absence of a revolution in Britain is not necessarily an embarrassment to orthodox Marxists who wish to support the more gradual transformation of capitalism envisaged in the neo-Marxist programme.

The major objectives of the programme are the nationalization of a number of the largest companies in the manufacturing sector, the extension of a limited version of planning to all the largest firms and measures to reduce the inequalities of wealth, particularly those accumulations arising from inheritance. The logic behind the programme is straightforward. There is reason to think that the largest firms, especially multinationals, have not acted in the interests of society as a whole. They have failed to invest in the face of uncertainty about the future; they have closed down plant without regard to the effects on workers; and they have taken state subsidies to maintain payments to shareholders. They need therefore to be made more accountable to their workforces and to society as a whole. The key to this is planning agreements between firms, the trade unions, and the government. All large firms would be involved in the exercise. They would prepare long term strategic plans for one to five years ahead. These plans would specify investment and production plans with their employment consequences, especially those involving redundancies and/or regional effects. The plan would then be subject to negotiation with the government and trade unions involved to reach agreement. Further nationalization is essential to this strategy. First, it would be necessary for the state to control the banking and insurance sectors to

[1] S. Holland *The Socialist Challenge* (Quartet Books, London, 1975).
[2] Avineri *op. cit.*

13

give the state a financial lever to use against recalcitrant companies. Second, nationalization would be an ultimate sanction against a firm, especially a multinational, which failed to comply with the planning agreement procedure. Third, twenty to twenty-five firms would be taken into public ownership. This would give the state direct control of a substantial part of the manufacturing sector. These enterprises could exercise oligopolistic leadership within their sectors, and hence 'pull up' the investments of the remaining private firms. Fourth, a National Enterprise Board could operate to create new public enterprises in sectors where the private firms are failing to take profitable opportunities. Lying behind the planning and nationalization strategy is a 'virtuous circle' theory of growth in the economy. The defect of capitalist enterprise is seen to be lack of investment, due to the capitalist phenomenon of falling profit rates identified by Marx. The difficulty is that each enterprise takes the current situation as given, and so is not prepared to respond. Suppose, however, that all firms *together* expanded investment and production. The investment would improve productivity enabling firms both to reduce prices (especially in export markets) and to increase wages. These in turn would generate the growth in demand to justify the intitial expansion in capacity and output. So a cumulative process of growth could be generated. The 'Planning Agreements' could serve to initiate this process. It should be noted that the system does not involve abandonment of the market in the allocation of resources. However it does seek to overcome a deficiency of information in the market system. Where the economy is dominated by a few large firms, the profitability of investment for one firm is critically dependent on the investment and production plans of other large firms. The planning system enables firms to assess prospects more accurately.

How would this system deal with the problems of worker alienation, which are a critical part of the neo-Marxist analysis? The solution is seen to lie in worker participation in the economic planning process, and in measures to reduce inequalities in wealth. Worker participation in economic decision-making is envisaged at all levels. Within the firm, worker control of management is preferred to the appointment of worker directors. Worker directors would tend to undermine the bargaining power of workers, would bring class conflict into the open in the board room, and could therefore enhance the sense of alienation. Worker control, with a worker's council appointing and controlling the management, would avoid these difficulties. Within the planning agreement system trade unions would have the power to influence the activities of large firms, particularly with regard to employment and redundancies. The trade unions are more likely to accept needed redundancies if there is a public-owned sector which is actively engaged in the provision of new employment on a regional basis, where it is most needed. Finally, the planning system would bring the trade unions into the processes of government in a more formal and detailed way, as they are involved in the formation of national economic policy and its translation into plans for the major enterprises, and on a regional basis.

Measures to reduce inequality would include more progressive income taxation, taxation of wealth and inheritance, and reduction in the level of income from property and shareholding. The last would be achieved by limiting payments to shareholders as part of the Planning Agreements with companies. More provision for social consumption goods is also part of the programme for greater equality. The hope is that greater equality in wealth would undermine the basis of class, and hence the class antagonism. It would also, together with trade union involvement in industrial decision-taking, reduce the militancy of the workers in asking for clearly inflationary wage demands.

(c) The Democratic Socialist Programme

The less avowedly Marxist analysis of the democratic socialists is matched by a less radical socialist programme. The emphasis shifts from the replacement of capitalism by a socialist system, to a modified capitalist system which Crossman[1] terms 'welfare capitalism'. The purpose is to intervene in the working of the capitalist system in order to improve its social performance. The political basis for action is a democratic socialist party which can draw support from all voters of good will, not exclusively the working classes. The middle classes are to be persuaded of the moral rightness of the programme, even if some aspects are not entirely in their class interests. The socialist party will, of course, draw considerable support from the trade unions, but it should not be dependent on them.

A particular feature of the programme is that nationalization is regarded as a policy tool which is to be used with caution. The case for public utilities is accepted. But in other sectors the prevailing market form is seen to be oligopoly rather than monopoly. If anti-monopoly policy is ineffective in these sectors, then 'competitive public ownership' of a part of the sector is a solution to maintain the competitiveness of the private firms. Similarly, it may be helpful to have a state bank in competition with the private banking sector. The emphasis in the public sector is to be on efficiency and profitability. Long term the public sector should contribute to public resources; it should not become dependent on subsidies. Within the firm the ideal is seen to be co-operation between all the workers in a common enterprise. There is little dogmatic prescription as to how this might be achieved, though industrial democracy is cautiously welcomed. But the hope of the neo-Marxists that nationalization will reduce the sense of alienation on the part of the workers is dismissed. Workers can be just as alienated by state capital as by private capital.

Planning is also given cautious treatment.[3] It is pointed out that 'planning' is already an internal feature of the large firms that operate in different secotrs of the economy. The question is whether this 'planning' needs supplementation to improve the performance of the

---

[1] R. H. S. Crossman 'Towards a Philosophy of Socialism' in Crossman (ed.) *New Fabian Essays* (2nd edition, London, 1972).

[2] E. F. M. Durbin *Problems of Economic Planning* (London, 1949).

[3] Durbin, *op. cit.* p.44.

private sector. Three areas are identified as requiring such supplementation. First, there may be sectors where private enterprise is not willing or able to accept the risks involved. This may be because of technological uncertainty: private finance is not likely to be available for very risky R and D for example. Or it may be related to extreme market uncertainty: if the market is subject to great fluctuations then private firms may be unable to maintain the level of capacity necessary to avoid supply constraints in the upswing of the trade cycle. Steel is sometimes thought to be such a sector. Second, there may be sectors where there is a definite divergence between the private and social costs. Planning processes can take into account social cost-benefit in assessing the proper levels of capacity and output. Third, planning may be related to the information defects that are perceived in the capitalist system. Durbin describes planning as 'the extension of the size of the unit of management, and the consequent enlargement of the field surveyed when any economic decision is taken'! Pooling of information and forecasts between the major firms in a sector, under the aegis of government, could lead to better investment decisions. The institutional form that this type of planning could take is exemplified by the operation of the economic development committees for a number of sectors set up under the umbrella of the National Economic Development Council in the late 1960s. Interestingly, Crosland[1] suggested in 1956 that in Britain the advantages of such planning are well recognized, but that the major difficulty is the lack of political will to make such planning work.

The above analysis concentrates on the supply side of the economy. However the democratic socialists are also committed to Keynesian macro-economic policy intervention on the demand side to ensure full employment. The forecasting of the economy, and the adjustment of fiscal and monetary instruments to keep aggregate demand in line with productive capacity, is as much part of the planning process as intervention on the supply side of the economy.

The social democratic analysis emphasizes the social disharmony caused by great disparities in income and wealth, rather than absolute poverty, as the main reason for redistributive taxation. The aspect of class conflict is again played down, except insofar as it is based on inequality. Apart from extensive provision for the economically disadvantaged—the old, the sick, the chronically unemployed, large families, or single parent families—the main emphasis is on taxation. Unearned income is to be taxed heavily: Crosland[2] envisages a situation where the return to shareholders will be reduced by taxation to a level commensurate with a 'fair' return on capital.[3] This is linked to the proposition that the 'surplus' above this level should be used to generate new investment rather than to swell the consumption of the rich. Presumably he has in mind an arrangement whereby the tax

[1] C. A. R. Crosland *The Future of Socialism* (Jonathan Cape, London, 1952) ch. 24.
[2] Crosland, *op. cit.* chapter 20.
[3] The calculation of a fair return, including a return for risk, is not, of course, a simple matter.

proceeds are diverted into productive investments via a state bank. Taxes on capital gains, capital transfers, and wealth are also advocated, to supplement the taxation on inheritance. The intention is to reduce the accumulations of wealth in individual hands, and to prevent new accumulations. On the other hand, saving for retirement, via private superannuation schemes, is to be encouraged.

As in most socialist programmes, extensive provision of public goods such as education, health, and other amenities, is seen as a redistributive device. It is also the basis for providing better life chances for the poorer sections of the community, particularly in education, which is seen as a major contributor to social mobility. On the other hand, Crosland[1] is concerned that equal opportunity should not merely provide a means for able children from the working class to escape into the middle class meritocracy, thus leaving the working class bereft of able leadership. But equal opportunity is seen by Crossman[2] as a tool for preventing the control of the state and the economy from falling into the hands of a self-perpetuating class (arising from the 'public' schools and Oxbridge). Preservation of strict meritocratic methods of appointment to top jobs is to be preferred.

Finally, we should note that Crosland[3], at least, is unwilling to countenance government intervention in the labour market, except in the most extreme inflationary circumstances. He admits the dangers of wage inflation and labour immobility in a full employment economy. But he argues that intervention would have to come to terms with the political fact of trade union autonomy and independence. He is not prepared to interfere with that: or at least he is not prepared to face the political consequences of trying to do so.

(d) The Questions for Ethical Discussion

In the preceding paragraphs we have set out, first, the socialist analysis of capitalism, and secondly, a description of a variety of socialist programmes. Our next task is to outline the major questions for ethical enquiry in the subsequent sections of this paper. We propose to circumvent what might be thought to be the next logical step, which is to ask whether the socialist analysis of capitalism (in any of its varieties) is *true.* One reason for avoiding the question is the observation that the nature of the analysis, and the results obtained depend to a large extent on the concepts which are used in the analysis. (Thus 'class', 'power', 'surplus', 'capital', 'property', 'equality', are all important concepts within the Marxist scheme. It should also be clear that these concepts are not ethically neutral: they are chosen because they are close to the ethical standpoint of the analyst. The degree of importance he attaches to them will be very different from those of an economic liberal, and he will see different types of social interaction as fundamentally important. For example, the Marxist will emphasize power in 'market' relations, the economic liberal will emphasize trade. This does not mean that we are entirely shut up in relativism in our social science. For the different paradigms can

---

[1] Crosland *op. cit.* chapter 10.
[2] Crossman *op. cit.*
[3] Crosland *op. cit.* chapter 21.

themselves be inspected for their logical and causal completeness, and their predictions tested against the real world in terms of their own concepts. For example, the simple Marxist predictions of a falling rate of profit and a progressive immiserization of the workers have not proved correct. The propositions that certain groups in society will have closely defined class interests, and that economic power is synonymous with political power, are clearly susceptible of further theoretical and empirical analysis. Presumably empirical failures should lead to a reconsideration of the theory: but we note that this is likely to be a re-appraisal *within* the Marxist paradigm and not necessarily a rejection of it. A final choice between paradigms will have to be made on the basis of its congruence with evidence.[1] But the very idea of congruence, in social science, is bound to include some evaluation of what it is that our analysis should be congruent with. At that point, ethical presuppositions enter again. An analysis of the ethical assumptions of the socialist system will not decide the issue of truth, but it will at least tell us whether it is an intellectual option for a Christian social analyst. A second reason for avoiding the question of truth is that it is not a prerequisite for evaluation of socialist programmes, which are the subject of our enquiry. It would of course be a strong plus for a programme if the underlying analysis of the socio-economic situation were found to be accurate. There is still the question of whether the various elements in the programme have been given a proper weight in responding to the injustices revealed by the analysis. But even without the analysis (which, surely, following Marx, needs to be of a concrete situation) we must ask whether the ethical presuppositions of both the analysis and the programme are right.

We have chosen six areas for discussion. These are not mutually exclusive, nor are they intended to be exhaustive. (1) We begin with the role of the state or government in socialist thought. In all varieties of the socialist analysis it is envisaged that the state will take an active part in the regulation of the socio-economic life of the economy. (2) This leads immediately to consideration of the socialist ownership of all or part of the means of production, and implications for private property. (3) Social ownership normally facilitates the regulation of the economy, and in particular enables economic planning to replace or supplement the market. The main issue here is the efficiency or otherwise of the planning mechanism in the allocation of resources. (4) The existence of social ownership and planning is often said to be inimical to fundamental human freedoms. We need to examine the truth or otherwise of this accusation, and to assess the weight which should be ascribed to 'freedom'. (5) Socialist programmes are also motivated by assertions about the nature of work in relation to human values. (6) Finally, a tenet of all socialist programmes is a belief in social and economic 'equality'. We need to examine this concept in relation to the reasons advanced for it by socialists.

These six areas will concern us for the rest of the paper.

[1] The introductions to *Capital* (Penguin edition), written by Ernest Mandel, give a Marxist view of the academic debate about the validity of Marxist theory. The text of Desai is also very helpful. See E. Mandel 'Introduction' to K. Marx *Capital* Vols I-II (Penguin (UK), 1976); M. Desai *Marxian Economics* (O.U.P., Oxford, 1979).

4. THE STATE

In all socialist analysis the state plays an important role in society. We have already seen that the Marxist utopian ideal of the 'withering away' of the state is to be interpreted as a diminution of the alienation of the citizen from the state, rather than its disappearance. So for all practical socialist analysis the state remains as an active organizer. It is the state which is involved in the direction of economic activity, in 'ownership' of the means of production, in the provision of public goods and in measures to redistribute income and wealth.

(a) Christian Conceptions of the State

The Christian doctrine of the state is by no means a settled theological issue. All we may do here is to present what we believe to be a majority view on the interpretation of the biblical material, noting different emphases in the material.[1] The issue is discussed most explicitly in Romans 13.1-7, but our analysis must be extended to include other material, notably in the teaching and experience of Jesus. In the Romans passage, Paul is continuing the theme of God's sovereignty in human affairs, which he has expounded in relation to sin and salvation in the first eleven chapters.[2] The question in chapter 13 is how the Christian should relate to the state. The answer is to see the state as one aspect of God's providence—his moral rule and ordering of the world. (There is a parallel with the teaching about conscience in chapter 2.) About the origins of the state there is theological disagreement. One line of argument takes it back to the creation story in Genesis 2. God is the sovereign ruler of the world, but he delegates authority to human beings. This is not a 'creation ordinance' divorced from the work of Christ, since Christ himself was involved in creation, The fall has disordered God's order, but not destroyed it. So it is still God's plan that man, even fallen man, should take responsibility for the rule of creation. Human rulers are God's representatives—men who by virtue of their position stand in God's place. This is made clear by a comparison of Romans 12.19, 20, where wrath is specifically reserved to God, and chapter 13.4, where the ruler is God's instrument to bring wrath on evildoers. A second explanation of the origin of the state is that of St. Augustine[1], interpreting the same basic biblical material. He argues that the dominion given to man in Genesis 2 is over creation (things) and not over other men. In their original nature men are subject to God alone, and not to one another, since relationships (marriage, family) are based on love and not on power. It was the fall, with the

---

[1] I have drawn on the following authors:

    O. Cullman *The State in the New Testament.*

    R. A. Markus 'Two Conceptions of Political Authority . . .' in *Journal of Theological Studies* 1965.

    H. Richard Niebuhr *Christ and Culture* (Harper and Row, New York, 1951).

    J. H. Yoder *The Politics of Jesus* (Eerdmans, Grand Rapids, Michigan, 1972).

    J. M. Bonino *Revolutionary Theology Comes of Age* (S.P.C.K., London, 1975).

[2] N. T. Wright Series of four articles on Romans 13.1-7 in *Third Way,* May and June 1978.

[3] St. Augustine *De Civitate Dei* XIX, 14, 15.

disordering of relationships between men, which made political authority necessary to avoid the anarchy and destruction which proceeds from a free rein given to human selfishness. The authority of the rulers is an authority delegated from God. The provision of the state is an act of common grace on the part of God. A third strand of interpretation links the authorities to the principalities and powers of Colossians 1.16 and 2.15. Caird[1] traces the teaching about the powers to its Old Testament roots in the idea that the gods of heathen nations came to be regarded as subordinate forces acting under Yahweh (e.g. Psalms 29 and 89 and Deuteronomy 32.8, 9.) Since the power of each ruler was thought to be related to the power of the nation's god, it was natural to identify the rulers as subordinate ultimately to God. Assyria, for example, is so described in Isaiah 10.5-15. If this identification can be carried over into New Testament thought, then it is possible to interpret Colossians 1.16 as seeing the origin of the powers in the creative purposes of God. They are fallen, but can still be used for good. in the providence of God. The state can still be described as a 'minister of God'.

The common theme in all three interpretations is that the state is seen as an instrument of God's providence for preventing anarchy in human affairs. This conclusion is only strengthened by consideration of the various attitudes of men and women of faith to *heathen* rulers in the biblical record.[2] In Jeremiah 29 the Jewish people are exhorted, and in the book of Esther are shown, to be good citizens co-operating with the secular state. Nehemiah depends on the higher authority of the king in his dealings with Sanballat, the local governor. Daniel's loyalty to God leads him to civil disobedience, but despite the opposition of the state to God he is still prepared to continue in its service. The life and teaching of Jesus strongly suggests the same pattern. Quite apart from his famous dictum 'Render to Caesar the things that are Caesar's . . .', and his acknowledgement that Pilate's power over him is 'given . . . from above' (John 19.11), it is clear[3] that he specifically rejected the Zealot option, which advocated rejection and confrontation with the Roman authorities. He uses the title 'Son of Man' in his public utterances, rather than more definite assertions of his Messiahship. Finally, Paul himself maintains his teaching about the state apparently in the face of his experience. It is clearly a problem that it was the rulers who crucified Christ: in 1 Cor. 2.7-8 he excuses them on the grounds of their ignorance. After illegal ill-treatment at Philippi (Acts 16.19.40), he merely reminds the rulers of their duty according to the law. He accepts their rightful authority. In Acts 25.11 he exercises his right of appeal to a secular authority. (The only puzzling passage in the Pauline corpus is his instructions to Christians to avoid recourse to the secular courts in 1 Cor. 5. However, that appears to refer specifically to disagreements between Christian brethren, which should be settled within the church.)

[1] G. B. Caird *Principalities and Powers* (O.U.P., Oxford (U.K. edition), 1967).
[2] D. J. A. Clines 'Social Responsibility in the Old Testament' in *Interchange* No. 20, 1976, pp.194-207.
[3] Cullman *op. cit.*

The doctrine of the state just outlined should serve to warn us against two alternative views. The first is that which identifies the state too closely with the work of God in the world. This tendency is apparent in Aquinas, who took the view that the authority of the state is grounded in the natural order of things. In Thomist theology[1] the state has the duty and the right to enforce Christian morality on its citizens, along the analogy of a father requiring obedience from his children. The rulers may restrict the freedom of individuals in their own interests. However, all too easily a state may usurp God's privilege of legislating for thoughts and motives, becoming itself the arbiter of what is ultimately good for man. At this point the scepticism of Augustine is a healthy corrective, with its awareness of the sinfulness and corruptibility of the state. However we must also avoid the second alternative, which sees the state and the exercise of political power as intrinsically evil or demonic. This leads to exaggerated fears of state control and loss of individual freedom.

We need to be more precise at this juncture as to the tasks which are entrusted to the state in the biblical scheme. The purely negative aspect of preventing anarchy and lawlessness has already been stressed above. God prefers an atheistic government to anarchy. However the state also has the positive task of creating justice among its citizens. The biblical concept of justice describes both a 'situation' and an activity. The 'situation' is a purpose for man in society (more on this below), which has been perverted by the fall. It will never be attained in this world, because the effect of sin is that human relationships are predicated on a degree of selfishness in man, and the use of power to attain selfish ends. It is however the task of the state to protect those who will suffer injustice thereby, and to redress wrongs. So justice becomes an activity—the activity of putting right a disordered or disproportioned state of affairs. This activity is guided by the ideal of what should be, without naively supposing that it can ever be brought about in a sinful world. Now a state can fail to fulfil its responsbilities either by failing to act to redress injustices, or by promoting the interests of one group in society, or by promoting its own self-interest. These are precisely the accusations levelled at the rulers of Israel and Judah on many occasions in their history (see for examples Amos 2 and 4 or Isaiah 1.10-26). It is for this reason that the state of Romans 13 can attract the fearsome denunciation of Revelation 13.

(b) The Socialist State

We may now apply this biblical analysis to the concept of the state envisaged by socialists. First we should note that a powerful interventionist state cannot be rejected solely because it is powerful. It is the way in which it exercises its power that matters, not the fact of power. So our concern must be with the content of the socialist programme and the means that the socialist state uses to achieve its ends. However that does not exclude us from being sceptical about the

---

[1] Markus *op. cit.*

ability of powerful states to remain uncorrupted in their use of power. We should not be sanguine about a powerful state which has cut itself off from any real political constraints in terms of responsibility and accountability to its citizens.[1] The tendency of the state to misuse its power has been used by Niebuhr[2] to argue for a 'democratic' system. In such a system, ideally, power should be widely dispersed in order to prevent the misuse of power by the state for its own ends. 'Man's capacity for justice makes democracy possible: but man's inclination to injustice makes democracy necessary'. We should note that this is a deduction from biblical premises, but it has no direct biblical support: on the contrary, in the Bible all kinds of régimes are taken for granted, and are accepted as the 'ministers of God', so long as they attend to their God-appointed task. They cannot be rejected *a priori.* However we are right to be suspicious, and may prefer a democratic socialist solution to a communist one in practice.

Second, we must condemn any state that sets itself up as a 'god', as the sole arbiter of what is good in society, and as an object of worship, in that it aspires to attract the total commitment and loyalty of the citizens. This has been true of facist régimes, and is certainly true of the state in many communist countries. In the latter instance, this is specifically linked to an atheist, anti-Christian, stance. However, we should be wary of assuming that socialist states *have* to adopt this stance: it is not a necessary part of even Marxist ideology. A socialist state is perfectly feasible without it.

Third, we might criticize socialist programmes for their class bias. Is this not a clear case of the state stepping down from its God-appointed role of promoter of justice for all groups in society to a much more partisan programme on behalf of certain limited sections of that society? In which case it ceases to be a minister of God, and becomes merely the most powerful faction in a society which is formally 'anarchic' i.e. without the rule of God's law? However we must distinguish those situations in which the authorities favour a particular group or class because they *are* that group, and those in which the authorities act on behalf of a particular group because they would not otherwise be justly treated by society. An example of the first was Amin's blatant favouritism towards Muslims, and particularly members of his own tribe, in Uganda. An example of the second could be the treatment of widows and their dependents in Britain. In much socialist analysis these distinctions are at best blurred. Marx, as we have seen, was moved by the oppression and exploitation of the workers that he detected in the nineteenth century capitalism, and that gave him the moral basis for his espousal of the working class. However we may suspect that in later socialist analysis the cause of the working class is championed simply because they are that class. For this reason the analysis of the democratic socialists is to be preferred to that of the neo-Marxists.

[1] Compare the warning of Samuel to the people of Israel when they asked for a king (I Samuel 8.10-18).

[2] R. Niebuhr *Moral Man and Immoral Society* (UK edition, S.C.M., London, 1963).

(c) The Liberal Critique of the Socialist State

It is often objected that the socialist state infringes personal liberties. The Christian concept of freedom is treated separately below, and compared with that advanced by liberals. However at this point we will take the liberal premise, follow through their argument concerning the state and then evaluate the liberal state with our analysis above. The liberal theory of the state was first developed by Locke[1] and has been given a sophisticated modern treatment by Nozick.[2] Locke begins with individuals in a state of nature, 'a state of perfect freedom to order their actions and dispose of their persons and possessions as they think fit, within the bounds of the law of nature, without asking leave, or dependency upon the will of any other man.' No one ought to harm another in his life, health, liberty, or possessions. If he does, the injured party may punish or exact compensation. At this point a number of basic inconveniencies about the 'state of nature' become apparent. Though the individual is free, he is also insecure against the invasion of his rights by others. He may have insufficient power to punish or exact compensation. Agreements freely entered into may prove difficult to enforce. Feuds may develop in the private settling of scores. These difficulties drive men into commonwealths (Locke) or protective associations (Nozick) to secure their rights. The protective association, according to Nozick, arises naturally out of a state of nature, even though no one intends it or tries to bring it about. But it is a minimal state with the following features: it establishes a legal framework for relationships between the citizens, it acts as an impartial judge in disputes, and it has the power to carry out its judgments, including the exaction of compensation. In these tasks it is entirely dependent on the consent of the members of the protective association, who have agreed to enter it on the basis of the predefined constitution. In Locke's analysis this includes a legislature, chosen and appointed by the members of society, who have powers to make laws within certain overriding constitutional constraints. They are to have no arbitrary power over life, liberty, or possessions, of individuals. They may act only on the basis of settled and agreed laws, which apply impartially to all citizens. Decrees are not acceptable. The legislature are not to take from any man any part of his property without his consent. (What about taxes to pay for common purposes e.g. the expenses of the protective association? Consent here is redefined as consent of the majority to the taxation). Finally the legislature cannot transfer power to any other hands.

Nozick sees these features arising by an 'invisible hand' process, from local protective associations to a dominant protective association, which is the minimal state, in that it includes all the citizens. He is mainly concerned with the rights of 'independents'—those who do not wish to join the association. First he argues that the protective association will have to prohibit the private enforcement of justice on

[1] John Locke *Of Civil Government: Book II: An Essay Covering the True Original, Extent and End of Civil Government.*
[2] R. Nozick, *Anarchy, State and Utopia* (O.U.P., Oxford, 1974).

the grounds that it is risky or unreliable in procedure. If there are too many independents, there is a non-negligible risk for everyone else that they will be unfairly punished by an independent, and they will therefore live in fear. Punishment has to be based on agreed procedures for determining guilt or damages. So the dominant association may find itself having to protect one of its members against an independent who has used an unreliable or unfair procedure, and who has punished one of the members against his will. The methods it choses for doing this are to prohibit independents from exercising self-enforcement of their rights (including the right to punish), and to compensate the independents by extending its own protective services to them. Thus the dominant association becomes a *de facto* monopoly, since it is the only institution in society which has the *power* to prevent others from exercising their right to punish. It is not a *de jure* power. We should note that Nozick rejects the free rider argument that independents should be compelled to join the protective association because they benefit from its existence.

Whatever the merits of Nozick's description of the 'invisible hand' process by which states are formed, it is clear that the minimal state so described is not consistent with the biblical view outlined previously. The minimal state is a *de facto* state deriving its authority solely from the consent of its members. The biblical state derives its authority from God. The minimal state is restricted to a narrow range of activities determined solely by the ceding of rights on the part of the citizens. It is mainly concerned with providing the framework for transactions between citizens, and with punishing infringements of absolute personal rights. The biblical state has a much more positive role in promoting *justice* in the society, not merely protecting rights. The liberal critique of the socialist state is not therefore a Christian critique.

5. PROPERTY

Socialism is frequently criticized, especially by economic liberals, for its abrogation of the rights of property. In this section, we will appraise this criticism in the light of biblical teaching about property. We will also take a critical look at the arguments advanced by the economic liberals. The essential features of 'property' are: (a) the right to dispose of or utilize the property as the owner sees fit, (b) the right to enjoy the services it gives. Thus, if I own a car, I have the right to determine its use, and the right to enjoy the transportation it offers. If I own a piece of land, I have the right to say how it shall be used, and I am entitled to consume the proceeds from that use.

(a) Biblical Teaching about Property

Our thesis is that the biblical material is best interpreted as requiring a concept of trusteeship or stewardship in relation to property.[1]

In Genesis 1.26-30 and 2.5, man is given dominion over nature to care for it, and to provide for his existence. The created order is part of God's gracious provision for mankind. The promise of continuing provision is re-iterated in the Noahic covenant (Genesis 8). It is also part of the teaching of Jesus in the Sermon on the Mount (Matthew 6.25-32). The Bible also makes it clear that God gives specific dominion to particular people or communities. An obvious example was the provision of the land for the Children of Israel.[2] The land belongs to God (Leviticus 25.23), but is given to Israel as an 'inheritance', and particular portions to each family or clan as a 'heritage'. The family land was inalienable and particularly should not be sold to foreigners. At the Jubilee, every fiftieth year, land was to be returned to its original owner. The same basic idea of trusteeship applies to other forms of property in the Torah. It is derived from God, and made legitimate by the discretionary powers over creation given to man by God. There is no *inherent* sanctity of property. Theft is prohibited as a violation of the trusteeship which has been assigned to a particular person. The penalties involve restoration of that stewardship. The concept of stewardship is explicitly endorsed in the parable of the stewards in Luke 19.11-27. The resources are delivered to the individuals as trustees, and each is required to give an account of his dealings. Those stewards who had done well were rewarded with greater trusteeships. We next need to consider the nature of the trusteeship. Clearly the trustees are accountable to God; but for whose benefit should the trusteeship be exercised? The biblical material insists that the benefit should accrue to mankind in general. The

---

[1] We shall be making considerable use of the useful biblical analysis of M. Hengel. (M. Hengel, *Property and Riches in the Early Church* (S.C.M., London, 1974)). However he explicitly dismisses the kind of interpretation we shall give as being not specifically Christian, but attributable to Judaism and Greek sources. But his interpretation omits the concept of man's dominion over creation, and fails to mention the parable of the talents in Luke 19.11-27. We attach considerable importance to these.

[2] C. J. H. Wright *What does the Lord require?* (Shaftesbury Project Paper).

creation is given for *all* mankind. The Torah exhorts the Israelites to provide for the weak, the fatherless, and even the stranger. Amos emphasizes the subordination of the right to property to the obligation to care for the weaker members of society.

In Jesus' own teaching and ministry there are two contrasting attitudes. The first is his radical criticism of property. In Luke 12.22-34 he urges his followers to eschew concern with possessions, and renounce all cares about their daily needs. He himself is described as having no possessions (Luke 9.58), and he urged his disciples, when they set out on a preaching mission, to make do with an absolute minimum (Luke 9.3). Furthermore his teaching emphasizes the *dangers* of possessions. It is impossible to serve God and mammon (Luke 16.13). The rich farmer is condemned for his selfish and thoughtless accumulation (Luke 12.16-21). The rich man who neglects Lazarus lying at his gates ends up in Hades (Luke 16.19-31). The rich young ruler is challenged to renounce his possessions and follow Jesus (Mark 10.24). On the other hand, Jesus did not lead an ascetic life. He was accused of enjoying the company of the wealthy: 'Behold a glutton and a drunkard, a friend of tax collectors and sinners' (Luke 7.34).

These two aspects can best be reconciled by the idea that possessions are not wrong in themselves, but in the way in which we regard them. If we regard them as *ours,* and cling to them for support, they become an obstacle to our true dependence on God. The true attitude for the Christian is to see possessions as entrusted by God for use in the service of others. This interpretation enables us to understand the 'love communism' of the early church, when the Christians in Jerusalem had all things in common. It was a direct expression of Jesus' teaching. As the church grew outside Palestine. It increasingly attracted converts from the wealthier classes in society, and the teaching of Jesus continued to be relevant. Selfish accumulation is vehemently condemned in James 2 and 5. The ideal in 1 Timothy 6.6-9 is contentment. In the second century A.D. the pattern became established: the rich were not condemned for their riches, but were exhorted to live modestly and distribute to the poor. This is the theme of *The Rich Man's Salvation* written by Clement of Alexandria late in the second century, and was the basis for the programmes for relief of poverty that became the mark of the Christian believers in the Roman world. The basis is that all we have comes from God as the owner. As he has shared his good things with us, so we must share with others.

(b) Property in the Socialist System

In applying this strand of biblical teaching to the critique of socialism we need to make fundamental initial distinctions between property rights in one's own person, property rights over consumer goods, and property rights over the means of production. It is important to note that none of the socialist programmes envisages the abolition of the first two rights. Given the range of opportunities and goods available to him, the individual in a socialist system can decide what work he is going to do, what career he will pursue, and what goods he will buy, including such capital items as private houses. (It is true that more radical communist systems have been proposed, but these are outside the mainstream of socialist thought, and attracted the scornful criticism of Marx himself, who thought them utopian). Of course, the range of opportunities in a socialist system may be limited deliberately by the planning authorities who are not disposed to offer some goods considered to be of low priority. But this is not necessarily any more restrictive than the range of goods offered by a capitalist system at the same stage of development.

It is in the area of property rights over the means of production that socialist systems are most distinctive. Some socialist programmes are more radical than others in this respect: the communist system does not permit private ownership of the means of production (though in practice this may be relaxed in some sectors, especially agriculture associated with small producers). The social democrats, at the other extreme, actively encourage a lively privately-owned productive sector, reserving social ownership to major public utilities and natural resources. However the scope of social ownership is not at issue here. The question is whether such ownership conflicts with the biblical teaching. Our tentative answer is that in principle it does not. Within a socialist system individuals will continue to exercise stewardship responsibilities e.g. in the control of a factory, in working a machine, or in tending a plot of land. In doing this they necessarily have to make a wide range of stewardship decisions, given that tasks and responsibilities within a productive system can only be assigned in a general form. Certainly, insofar as the staff and workers are concerned, there will be little difference in stewardship responsibilities between a given factory located in a socialist system and that located in a capitalist society. However, there is a difference at the level of the management and direction of the firm. In a capitalist system the managers are able to decide the overall direction of the firm, e.g. in which markets it will operate, and how its activities will develop. It is this freedom of action which is restricted within a planned system. In effect the managers become agents of the planning board.[1] They are in receipt of instructions about what to produce, and even what inputs they may use. How this operates is the subject of our next section, when we will discuss questions of efficiency. These instructions have the important implication that the stewardship of the managers is exercised *in principle* for others, ideally to contribute to the well-being of the society as defined by the planners. By contrast, in capitalism, the stewardship of the managers is, in principle, directed to the interests of the owners. In practice, all these statements are too strong: the managers will have their own objectives, and may ally themselves to the interests of other groups, in particular their own staff, whether they operate in a capitalist or a socialist system. So the issue shifts away from the exercise of stewardship *per se,* which is more or less common to both systems, to broader questions about the right of the state to direct the allocation of resources, which was discussed in the previous section, and about the efficiency of the socialist allocation mechanisms, which is the subject of the next section. We have

---

[1] We note that this is equivalent to being a manager of a factory or subsidiary or a multinational enterprise.

27

established that stewardship is compatible with socialism; on one hand its scope may be more restricted, but the idea of stewardship of resources for others is fundamental.

However, the discussion so far has avoided what for many are the fundamental questions about property. First, should the state *own* property? Second, under what conditions, if any, is it right for the state to abrogate the existing property rights of individuals in the means of production e.g. by nationalization? These questions are in fact linked, and we will deal with them in turn.

The first question loses some of its polemic content if we rephrase it as follows. Is there any ethical objection *per se* to resources being allocated within society by a bureaucratic planning process, with stewardship being exercised by individuals, in conformity with what the political authorities conceive to be the interests of society? We have already seen that this does raise ethical issues, but they are not issues about ownership *per se*. Once again the questions are the role of authorities in society, and the efficiency of such bureaucratic systems. The rephrasing of the first question gives us a way into the second. We can now understand a move such as nationalization as removing the stewardship of certain blocks of resources from one set of stewards (the owners in a capitalist system) and entrusting those resources to a new set of stewards. Given the biblical emphasis on responsible stewardship and on the right to exercise that stewardship, we shall require very strong reasons for abrogating an existing stewardship right and transferring it to someone else. A number of possible reasons present themselves. The stewardship may not have been acquired by legitimate means e.g. it was accumulated by force or by some other unjust action. The stewardship is being exercised for purely selfish objectives, without regard to the detriment to others. For example, monopolization of a natural resource, and the deliberate restriction of supply to maximize private gain could be an example of this. Finally, stewardship may be incompetent, in the sense that the individual is incapable of exercising his rights because the resources are too large or too complex for his personal abilities. The case would be particularly strong in a situation where others are prevented from exercising stewardship by inadequate access to resources. A good example is afforded by land owners in a number of Latin American countries, who have shown themselves incapable or unwilling to use their land productively, and yet exclude competent peasant farmers from access to land. The first two of these reasons are those most frequently advanced by socialist writers to justify dispossession of existing property holders. However we may doubt whether a general condemnation of all capitalist ownership under these heads is justified. So, while we would not deny to the authorities the power to redistribute stewardship in order to promote justice in society, we should be cautious about accepting any general redistribution policy. We may well suspect that such a policy is motivated more by a desire to promote the interests of a new class against the old, rather than by the pursuit of greater justice.

(c) The Liberal Theory of Property Rights

The liberal theory of property rights has not been adduced in support of our argument, but, as it is often espoused in defence of private property, it needs our attention here to compare it and contrast it with the arguments developed above. The liberal theory is based on a natural rights doctrine which has two important presuppositions. The first refers to justice in acquisition. Locke[1] imagines an original state of nature in which there are no property rights. But every man does, of course, have rights over his own person. By his own labour he wrests from nature a patch of land for cultivation, or some other natural resource. Thereby he establishes a property right in that piece of nature. 'It hath by this labour something annexed to it that excludes the common right of other men.' 'God, by commanding to subdue, gave authority to appropriate'. The second presupposition is justice in transfer. After the initial phase of acquisition, individuals enter freely into exchanges, or make gifts, e.g. bequests to children. Over a period of time these actions, together with the action of chance factors e.g. good and bad harvests, may well generate inequalities. But so long as justice in acquisition and justice in transfers have been observed, then the 'natural rights' which emerge as a result of the historical process of acquisition and exchange are vindicated.

This argument attracts a number of critical comments. First, the Lockean notion of the pioneer wresting his plot of land from the virgin nature is more romantic than apposite. Very few new assets are created as the outcome of *one* person's labour. Second, there is every reason to believe the present distribution reflects at least some previous injustices in transfers. Even if we could somehow ensure that all future transfers were just, since the starting point would be unjust so would the outcomes of continuing historical process. Third, a Christian critique of the liberal theory would dissent from the emphasis on property rights, implying use for one's own ends, and would emphasize stewardship rights, implying use for the good of society in general. Fourth, the jubilee provisions of the Law specifically abrogated the rights created by transfers on equal terms (Leviticus 23). The regulations concerning the year of jubilee emphasize that God gave the trusteeship of particular areas of land to particular families. Over a period of years, in a predominantly agricultural community, it was likely that some families would lose control over their land by incurring debts. However at the end of seven sabbath years i.e. after forty-nine years, there was to be a jubilee year in which all land was restored to its original owners. They were the trustees appointed by God for that land, and it was to be returned to them. (An indication of how seriously this family trusteeship was viewed was the refusal of Naboth to cede his vineyard to Ahab in 1 Kings 21). We may note too that the original allocation of land, and the provision of the jubilee, were a powerful instrument for promoting equality and for ensuring that each family had access to resources so as to be able to exercise stewardship. We will return to these themes below.

---

[1] John Locke *Of Civil Government: Book II*. Compare the modern restatement in R. Nozick *Anarchy, State and Utopia* (O.U.P., Oxford, 1974).

6. PLANNING AND EFFICIENCY

(a) The Definition of Efficiency

In Genesis 1.26-30 and 2.15 man is given charge over the natural order to care for it and, to provide for his existence. A variety of words is used to give content to this charge. First we note that man is made in the image of God. In the ancient Near East it was the custom for a king to erect an image of himself in a subject territory as a visible sign of his dominion. Hence man in God's image is a sign of God's sovereignty over his creation. Man is God's steward. His role is defined by some very strong words: 'dominion' (v.26), 'subdue' (v.28), in the Hebrew both imply not only dominion, but also dominion for use. This emphasis is balanced in Chapter 2 by language which implies care for the creation. Thus the man is put in the garden to till it and to keep it, and his relation to the animals is described by his action in naming them (Chapter 2.19, 20), suggesting that they are recognized as having independent value and existence, apart from the use that man could make of them. In the aftermath of the flood, God makes a promise to maintain the natural cycles of day and night, summer and winter, seedtime and harvest (Genesis 8.22), as a parallel to the creation narrative. Noah is then enjoined to replenish and subdue the earth, to be fruitful and to enjoy the fruits. But again the language of dominion is matched by the language of respect and care, especially for the animals. Their flesh may be eaten, but not with the blood, which signifies the life of the animal (Chapter 9.4). The animal has value in and of itself, and its life is not to be taken thoughtlessly or wantonly.

The fundamental economic problem, that of the proper utilization of scarce resources, can now be set in a biblical framework. The use of such resources for the satisfaction of human needs is permitted but there is also a Christian imperative to use natural resources economically. That is, they are to be used efficiently, without waste. Efficiency and waste can be defined in the usual sense of economic efficiency, which is minimizing the use of resources to achieve a given end. But to this should be added particular attention to minimizing damage to the natural order of a kind that cannot be restored or remedied. Thus a process that destroys or has some other irreversible effect (e.g. pollution of the atmosphere) in the natural order should be avoided, however 'efficient' it may be, technically or economically. We should also note that efficiency can only be defined in respect of given ends or objectives. The utilitarian definition sets no limit to man's wants, which require satisfaction. So there is a tension between unlimited wants and scarce resources. Whether or not this is an accurate description of the psychology of fallen man, it is clearly contrary to the biblical norm, which would see the use of natural resources, and the animal world, as limited to human needs. The definition of needs is not easy, of course, and we will have to return to the question in the section on equality. But the present discussion does highlight an issue of fundamental importance for the analysis of 'efficiency'. That is, efficiency can only be defined in respect of given ends. Two examples may serve to illuminate this point. In his work on famines, A. K. Sen[1] has found that in a number of famine areas food was actually being shipped out of the area while the inhabitants were dying. The proximate cause of the famine was the inability of the poor to buy the food, because unemployment or underemployment or some other economic affliction had left them with insufficient means. Hence the markets had 'worked' in the sense of shipping out the food to other areas where demand was backed by ability to pay. In one sense the markets 'worked efficiently', moving foodstuffs from markets where effective demand was too small to areas where it was greater. But in terms of distributing food to those who needed it, it was clearly inefficient. A second example is afforded by the experience of many visitors to socialist economies. They report adversely on the shortage of consumer goods, and the queues for them in the stores. However, their conclusions as to the 'inefficiency' of socialist systems are beside the point if in fact the shortages resulted from deliberate decisions taken by the planners. For example, the planners may have given low priority to consumer goods, and may regard rationing by queuing as more just than rationing by price, as a method of distributing the limited quantities. Exactly the same situation arose in Britain during the Second World War when resources were deliberately diverted to the war effort, reducing the supplies of some goods to the consumer. It was an act of policy by the authorities which gave rise to the shortages. The 'efficiency' of the situation has to be evaluated in terms of the ends desired.

(b) The Efficiency of Planning

The efficiency of planning as a means of allocating the resources of an economy was the subject of and intense technical debate in the economics literature of the mid 1930s.[2] The burden of the critics' argument was that a planned system worked without competitive markets in which prices could be set. Hence economic rationality was impossible, for there would be no independent valuation of different outputs. Hence, *a priori*, inefficiency was bound to result. Hayek[3] also drew attention to the need for information in any planning system. Abandoning the price system implied a loss of information about the needs of society which could not be obtained by other means. He argued that the technical expertise required for planning a whole economy was unimaginable. The size of the problem in terms of the number of final and intermediate goods, and the production links between them, defied the calculating capacity of any group of planners. The problem was just too big to solve. Lange[4] assumed the use of the price system for the distribution of consumer goods, and for making

---

[1] A. K. Sen 'Starvation and exchange entitlements' in *Cambridge Journal of Economics* (1977, vol. 1) pp.33-35.

[2] The main critics were von Mises, von Hayek and Lionel Robbins. See: L. von Mises in F. A. von Hayek (ed.) *Collectivist Economic Planning* (London, 1935); F. A. von Hayek 'Socialist Calculation: The Competitive "Solution" ' in *Economica* (1940, vol. 7) pp.125-149; L. Robbins *The Great Depression* (London, 1934).

[3] F. A. von Hayek 'The use of knowledge in society' in *American Economic Review* (vol. 35, 1945).

[4] Lange responded to their criticisms in two articles. See: O. Lange, 'On the economic theory of socialism' in *Review of Economic Studies* (1936-37).

payments to labour. Intermediate goods were to be planned by the central planning board. He then showed that even in the absence of markets the planners could establish prices by a trial-and-error method. He particularly rejected the criticism that a planned system would require planning of each individual's work and consumption. The law of large numbers operates to give stable aggregates in consumption. Hence the planning board only needs to know the distribution of income, and average consumption patterns.

The debate of the 1930s gave rise to a substantial technical literature on the theory of planned economies, which has been stimulated by the observed experiences of planning experiments in socialist and communist countries. Three models of the socialist economy have been developed.[1]

(i) **The bureaucratic centralized model.** There is a hierarchical system of planning and management, with a central planning authority (CPA) at its apex. The plan specifies physical production targets by sectors which are then progressively broken down into sub-sectors and finally plant production targets. The internal consistency of a plan is determined by the method of material balances i.e. by summing all the requirements for an intermediate good, and then adjusting the targets for the supplying sector. The planning proceeds by a process of iteration until a consistent plan is found. It may be that no detailed plan is feasible, in which case the sectoral targets have to be adjusted. For example, a plan for construction could require more cement than the cement sector was capable of supplying within the plan period. Final goods are allocated to consumer by a mixture of prices, rationing, and rationing-by-queueing. This system suffers from its information needs. In the USSR some 20,000 commodities are included in the central plan. Beyond this, detailed instructions have to be given to each plant about its production targets, and its sources of inputs.

(ii) **Planometric centralist models.** The economy is viewed as a huge input-output model, with flows between sectors calculated on the basis of the technology in use. The model is solved on a computer, enabling the calculation of an optimal plan, given the objectives fed in. Constraints on the system can be built into the model. The computer can also calculate implicit prices for inputs and outputs, which are given to plants in place of physical targets. Each plant then has to meet financial targets calculated in terms of the plan prices. These prices need not be the same as the consumer prices, which may be adjusted to bring demand into line with the supply that is planned.

[1] See Ellman, Heal and Wilczynski as follows:
    (a) M. Ellman 'Optimal planning' in *Soviet Studies* 20 (1968).
    (b) M. Ellman *Soviet Planning Today* (Cambridge University Press, 1971).
    (c) G. M. Heal *Theory of Planning* (North Holland, 1973) Chapter 3.
    (d) J. Wilczynski *The Economics of Socialism* (George Allen and Unwin, London, 1977) Chapter 2.

(iii) Selectively decentralized model. The computational problems involved in planometric models require a very sophisticated and powerful computing facility. In the absence of such a facility, a rather less sophisticated planning system can be evolved. This involves the setting of provisional prices, the reporting back by the plants of their production intentions given those prices, the scrutiny of the replies for inconsistencies between sectors, and the consequent adjustment of prices until a solution is found. The system may even be extended to investment by specifying a rate of interest or profit on the installation of new equipment, and adjusting the rate to bring intended investment into line with the supply capacity of the capital goods sector.

Within these three options we may distinguish two types of decentralization. The first is information decentralization, in terms both of information flowing from the central planning authority to the firms, and *vice versa.* More information incurs three disadvantages: (a) errors in transmission (b) errors in computation (c) deliberate misinformation. The first two are clear enough. The third refers to the possibility that the firm will provide false information about itself to the CPA in an attempt to reduce the production targets determined for it. For example, a plant may give false information about its production capacity and its input requirements to avoid an imposed target which would put a strain on the plant. These disadvantages are all reduced as one moves from the bureaucratic physical planning model to the decentralized model, though the latter does not eliminate the possibility of deliberate misinformation, which has to be dealt with by incentives. The second aspect is the decentralization of decisions, which deserves some detailed discussion. The matter can be illustrated by consideration of the principal-agent 'problem'. The principal (in this case the CPA) is seeking to ensure that the behaviour of the agent (in this case the managers of plants) accords with the wishes of the principal. There are three solutions. In the first the principal gives the agent detailed instructions as to how he is to act. In the second, the principal lays down guidelines as to how the agent is to act, but leaves the detailed decisions to the agent. In the third, the agent is given performance indicators by which he will be judged (and to which incentives may be attached). It is then up to him to take decisions. The choice between these modes of principal-agent relations is determined by various considerations. It is clear that the interests of the principal and the agent will diverge, not least because the principal only has to *say* what he wants, while the agent has to exert himself to achieve those objectives. The agent thus will trade off the objectives for a bit more leisure. This would appear to indicate that the first relationship— that of detailed instructions to the agent—will be the most advantageous. However two considerations militate against this. The first is the question of information and monitoring. The principal has to convey much more information to the agent, and he has to know a great deal about the capacity of the agent. Further the activity of the agent will have to be monitored closely to see if he is obeying instructions. Given that information giving and receiving is costly (time-consuming), there are likely on this count to be reasons for adopting the method of performance indicators linked to incentives. A further consideration is the location of blame if things go wrong. If the agent is given detailed instructions, and performance is unsatisfactory, it is very difficult in an uncertain world to know whether the instructions were at fault, or the environment was less favourable, or whether the agent did not make any effort. The particular point is that the agent has no incentive to exert himself, as he can always shift the blame.[1] If, on the other hand, the agent is evaluated solely on the basis of the performance indicators, it is up to him to produce a good result, and he can be blamed for failures. Applying this analysis to alternative relationships between the planning board and the firm it is clear that both decentralized information and decentralized decision-taking are likely to be favoured.

The principal-agent framework is also useful for understanding the question of incentives. It is first worth noting that all socialist systems have in practice retained the usual pattern of incentives found in market economies for workers below the level of management. Positive economic incentives are represented by wages, bonuses, and promotion prospects. Negative economic incentives are the threat of dismissal and the possible reduction in earnings. There are also the important non-economic incentives of 'doing a good job', 'working for the good of a group of workmates' etc. So the problem of incentives has to be located at the level of management. Now the principal-agent theory does indeed predict that a physical planning system will find it difficult to ensure that plant managers are efficient. It was precisely this difficulty which led the USSR to adopt the Liberman proposals in 1965.[2] Liberman emphasized the need to provide performance criteria for enterprises by which managerial performance could be evaluated. The criterion chosen was profit, defined as revenue minus costs of production, where the prices of outputs and inputs are determined by the CPA and not by the enterprise. Incentives were then attached to profit performance. A more radical decentralization would involve enterprises financing themselves by loans from state banks at given interest rates and repayment terms, and thus being able to determine their size in the long run. But prices would remain determined by the CPA.

The problem of incentives seems to be greatly overstated by the critics of socialism. The separation of ownership and control in large firms in capitalist economies has brought a parallel problem of how to give incentives for efficiency to professional managers, given that they do not usually have ownership rights over the profits.

[1] This is the phenomenon of 'moral hazard' in insurance contexts, which gives rise to 'excess clauses'. Total damage insurance gives no incentive to the driver to avoid minor bumps in his car.

[2] A good summary of Liberman's views is available in English in E. G. Liberman 'Profitability and Socialist Enterprises' in *Problems of Economics* (March 1966) pp.3-10.

We have avoided, so far, the question of what determines the allocations made by CPA as between sectors. In practice, socialist planning boards have shown marked preferences for accumulation rather than consumption, and within consumption, for social goods rather than private ones. Thus 20%-30% of national output is allocated to accumulation. Within accumulation priority is given to the means of production. Up to 30% of total consumption is directed to social consumption goods—child care, education, provision for old people, housing, public transport. The effect of these priorities has been a restriction on the quantities of private consumption goods available, which has led to shortages and rationing. But this has been a deliberate act of policy: the long run needs of society have been put first, and consumption has taken second place. However there has been a trend for socialist planners to pay more attention to consumer demand in response to the discontent generated by too long a period of attention to other needs.

This role of the CPA was criticized by Hayek.[1] In the absence of an ethical consensus concerning such allocations, it would be impossible to get everyone to agree on the criteria for the division between current and future consumption, and between private and social consumption. Hence, according to Hayek, planning cannot be 'democratic', and truly reflect the wishes of the people. Even in its own terms this criticism is curious, since democracy does not necessarily demand that *everyone* agrees to a particular course of action. Moreover, from a Christian standpoint, it fails to accord to the authorities the power to act to promote justice in society. Given that right for the authorities, the argument against planning *per se* is without foundation. That is not to deny that CPAs may use their powers in ways that fail to respond to the needs of the population, and are plainly unjust. This is particularly the case when the needs of the State machine dominate.

(c) Planning to Supplement the Market System

Before we leave the subject, we need to consider planning as a supplement to the market system. The Yugoslav system was described above in section 3(a), and the idea of planning agreements in section 3(b). Unfortunately there is no substantive evidence as to the efficiency of such systems. The Yugoslav experiment has been the subject of considerable debate in the economics literature. Not least it is an interesting case as one can compare different régimes of economic organization in which economic growth has occurred: full capitalism, central planning, limited sectoral planning, and market economy with labour-managed firms. Unfortunately it is not easy to disentangle the effects of economic organization from other factors affecting the rate of growth in a given period. The 'planning agreements' system has not been put into practice, though there is some experience of indicative planning in France. The purpose of planning to supplement the market system was succinctly described by Durbin[2] as an 'extension of the size of the unit of management and the consequent enlargement of the field

[1] F. A. von Hayek *The Road to Serfdom* (London, 1944).
[2] E. F. M. Durbin *Problems of Economic Planning* (London, 1944).

surveyed when any economic decision is taken'. This principle is unobjectionable: the whole range of consequences of any decision should be taken into account. But it avoids the question of how the decisions should be taken. The objection is put in its crudest form by those who would say that a 'bunch of civil servants' would not be capable of running a complex industry. This can be broken down into two separate objections. One is that it would be impossible to find civil servants with the skills required, which is absurd. The second is that the control mechanism and informational complexity would render the whole effort inefficient. This returns us to the problems of control and information that we have discussed above, in the context of fully planned systems.

Some indication of the difficulties of creating control mechanisms can be gleaned from the experience of the U.K. nationalized industries. The 1967 White Paper[1] on the control of the nationalized industries tried to lay down specific economic criteria by which the management of public industries was to make decisions. The idea was to enable the managers to act independently, without constant recourse to the sponsoring ministry in Whitehall. A study in 1974[2] showed that this objective had not been attained. The economic criteria were not operationally effective, and successive governments had interfered with the decision-taking process. The assessment of the system was also made more complicated by the fact that several nationalized industries—notably coal, steel, and the railways—faced severe structural problems, usually arising from excess capacity. Management problems were exacerbated by the strong Trades Unions existing in these sectors, and by the clear political impact of decisions that had to be considered e.g. pit closures and redundancies. On the other hand a number of nationalized industries with growing markets, especially gas, electricity, and telecommunications, had an enviable record of productivity growth in the 1960s and 1970s. The 1978 White Paper[3] recognized the difficulties of the previous system in two ways. First it abandoned the attempt to set criteria for decisions that would include social costs and benefits, as opposed to direct financial criteria. Second, it provided for direct political assessment of the consequences of the corporate plan for each industry. It remains to be seen whether this system will be any more effective.

[1] *Nationalised Industries: A Review of Economic and Financial Objectives* (1967) Cmnd. 3437 (London).
[2] National Economic Development Office *A Study of UK Nationalised Industries* (1976).
[3] *The Nationalised Industries* (1978) Cmnd. 7131 (London).

7. FREEDOM

One of the most influential critiques of socialism was F. A. Hayek's *The Road to Serfdom* published in 1944.[1] In that book and his subsequent writing, Hayek has argued the case that freedom can only survive in a liberal free-market economy, and that socialism is *per se* inimical to human freedom. It is a theme that was powerfully restated by Milton Friedman[2], and has become central to the critique of socialism. In this section we consider Christian ideals of freedom first, before making an assessment of the threat to freedom posed by socialism, as described in the writings of economic liberals. It will also serve to distinguish Christian and liberal concepts of freedom.

(a) Biblical Anthropology and the Concept of Freedom

At first sight, the biblical material on human freedom is not encouraging. The existence of slavery is accepted in the Old Testament, without adverse comment. In the New Testament, Paul exhorts slaves to be subject to their master, and restricts his advice to the masters that they are to treat slaves with consideration, remembering that both masters and slaves are subject to the same heavenly Master, who shows no partiality (Ephesians 6.5-9). In the case of the runaway slave, Onesimus, Paul urges Philemon to take him back, without suggesting any change in his status. However this permissive attitude to the formal institution of slavery is confounded by consideration of some of the detailed teaching on the subject. For example, Deuteronomy 23.15-16. requires that a runaway slave should not be returned to his master, but should be free to live in a town of his choosing. He is in no way to be oppressed. Furthermore, provision was made for slaves to be paid a fair wage as workers, and conditions for manumission were laid down. The effect of these provisions, if they had been applied, would have been the abolition of slavery as an institution. The slave who was treated badly could simply leave and obtain his freedom. Paul exhorts Philemon to treat Onesimus as a 'beloved brother', which scarcely suggests the continuation of a master-slave relationship.

Personal freedom is also a part of the Messianic vision of Isaiah 61 which Jesus quotes with approval in Luke 4.18-19; 'The spirit of the Lord is upon me . . . He has sent me to proclaim release to the captives . . . to set at liberty these who are oppressed'.

The Bible emphasizes human free will in the choice between good and evil. The responsibility for human sin is laid on all who are in Adam. As Romans 1-3 argues, every man has both a knowledge of the truth, and the responsibility for rejecting it. He also has the responsibility and freedom either to accept or to reject the gift of God's grace offered in Christ. He is a responsible moral being not merely a creature.[3]

---

[1] F. A. von Hayek *The Road to Serfdom* (London, 1944).

[2] M. Friedman *Capitalism and Freedom* (University of Chicago, 1962).

[3] This is not an appropriate place to discuss the doctrine of predestination in Reformed thought from Calvin to Karl Barth. But that doctrine appears to limit his freedom even in the critical respect of accepting or rejecting God's grace.

Another theme of biblical teaching on freedom concerns freedom from sin. The clearest statement is in the Pauline teaching, especially in Romans 6 where Paul describes the sinner as a slave to sin, unable to keep the law, and unable to please God. In Christ, and through his atoning death, the sinner is delivered from his slavery to sin, and is enabled to live a new life of freedom, free to do God's will perfectly. The Christian becomes a 'slave of God'. However chapters 12-14 make it clear that the new freedom which a man has in Christ has its practical consequences in a life of service to others, both within the Christian community and without. Personal liberty is to be sacrificed in order not to be an offence to others (chapter 14).

It is not evident that freedom in the theological sense has much to do with the more secular concept of freedom in society that we are discussing in this section, except that it reminds us of the very high value that God puts on human beings. That God should treat us as responsible agents suggests very strongly that we should extend the same respect to our fellow human beings. But as far as freedom in society is concerned, the biblical material emphasizes strongly duties and obligations to our fellow men. The key to this is that the Bible sees man as a social being, not as an individual. Adam is created in social fellowship with God (who is himself plural in the Trinity). This fellowship is supplemented by the provision of Eve. As sinners we all share in the race of Adam, of fallen man. The grace of God is extended first to a family, which becomes a nation, the people of Israel. Membership of that people involves relationships of obligation which are strongly emphasized in the law. The grace of God is then extended to a new people of God, the church. That new people is described in an organic relation to one another, as the body of Christ. As Christians we are part of a new race, in Christ. Our dependence on one another is strongly emphasized. The conclusion must be that *ideal* humanity finds its expression not in individualism, but in membership of one another. It is the fall that generates self-seeking behaviour and which disrupts human relationships of love and trust. However this argument must not be pushed to the point of attributing all expression of human freedom to sinfulness. The correct model is of responsible individuals entering into loving relationships and accepting responsibilities within those relationships i.e. loving one's neighbour as oneself. Sin has perverted this scheme by tilting the balance in the direction of individualism, and by emphasizing power and domination in relationships in place of love, trust, and mutual responsibility.

We may draw from this teaching three related themes which are relevant to the consideration of freedom within a society. The first theme is that individual freedom to act is likely to lead, if unchecked, to some individuals having power over others, and to a failure to accept responsibilities towards other human beings. The second theme follows from this. The power of some individuals inevitably restricts the freedom of others. Hence it may be no contradiction to argue simultaneously for more restrictions on the freedom of those who are powerful, and for less restrictions on the freedom of the weak. Freedom then, is not an end in itself, though it will be highly valued by the Christian. It must be taken in conjunction with its other consequences, particularly the lack of responsibility that it engenders in sinful men. Where freedom is restricted, we need to ask why it is restricted, and what the consequences of absence of restrictions would be. A third theme is that we should not treat freedom as an abstract ideal. We need to distinguish different types of freedom. Thus, freedom to worship God, or to love another person, is not likely to be in dispute. But economic freedom is more open to discussion. For example, in a market capitalist system, the freedom of the capitalist to make workers redundant is not matched by an equal freedom to work on the part of the worker who faces unemployment.

(b) Does Socialism restrict Freedom?

For many people the question, 'does socialism restrict freedom?' has an obvious response. The dramatic warnings of Solzhenitsyn, and the experience of communist régimes in various parts of the world, serve as a grim reminder of the power of socialist régimes to oppress their people, especially if they are members of dissident minorities. However that experience is not unique to totalitarianism régimes of the Left. It has been the experience of fascist régimes in Europe, military régimes in South America, and of the majority of Islamic states. The first two, at least, have been associated with capitalist economic organization, though with varying degrees of state intervention in the market. Totalitarian régimes are by no means unique to socialism. However that does not exclude the possibility that socialism may be particularly conducive to such régimes.

This point is argued forcefully by Hayek.[1] The goals of socialism are ideals of social justice, equality and security. These are to be sought by the creation of a planned economy (or in democratic socialism, by the creation of a substantial planned sector in the economy). So planning is not just rational decision-taking: it is the setting down of a rational plan for controlled social change. Since no complete ethical code is available, and since individual views of what should be done are likely to coincide in only a very limited area, democratic planning becomes impossible. The plan either stands or falls as a whole. It is not open to being scrutinized section by section, or to being broken down. So no true agreement is likely to be achieved in a democratic society. Planning is delegated to experts, who have discretion to choose both the goals and the means of achieving them.

Hayek disposes of the defence of planning which argues that it applies to only part of life, which if implemented successfully would leave men free for higher things. He argues that there is no separate 'economic motive'. People are motivated by a desire for general opportunity, by the desire for power to achieve unspecified ends. Almost all choices do involve economics in that the means to achieve ends are provided by our fellow men. So planning *would* impinge in restricting the range of possibilities. For example, the planner can restrict the range of choice

[1] von Hayek *op. cit.*

of different consumer goods. He can control occupational choice by fixing qualifications and remuneration for each kind of work. The appearance of choice would be deceptive because there would be no scope for the individual to branch out on his own, to 'prove himself'. Furthermore, as Friedman has pointed out, a socialist régime gives little scope for dissenters to obtain a hearing for their ideas. There will be few wealthy patrons who can espouse a political cause. Even if the dissidents can raise the money, they may be unable to get their literature printed or purchase space in the media. Finally, since the only source of employment is the state, the planners dispose of a particularly powerful sanction against dissent.

What Hayek has shown is that government in a socialist planned economy has the potential to be totalitarian, but this is far from establishing that it has to be, unless one holds that all power corrupts, and one must therefore expect the full potential of any system to be exploited by sinful men. As we have already seen, the planning mechanism does affect the allocation of resources between different sectors of the economy, but it need not impinge on individual choices in consumption, work and leisure. In practice, there are few socialist systems which have attempted to impinge on such choices. The reasons, which have to do with the information bases of planning, have been described in the previous section. A similar response can be made to Hayek's general point, that a less privileged position for an individual in society is easier to accept when it is the result of chance, than when it is the outcome of the determination of some planning authority. Hayek extols the virtues of a system in which the authorities announce the 'rules of the game' beforehand, enabling each individual to order his life in the light of those rules, without *ad hoc* (and *ad hominem*) action by the authorities. But in practice, no socialist planning mechanism has ever determined the pattern of life of particular individuals, and there are good reasons (lack of information) why it should not do so. The persecution of dissident individuals and groups in communist countries can be attributed to totalitarianism, not to socialist planning.

As we shall see below, Hayek's basic objection is to the state determining objectives for resource allocation, which do not reflect the consensus of all the citizens. But this is effectively to remove from the authorities the right to act as God's ministers to redress injustices. As we have already observed that may well involve restricting the freedom of the strong, in order to promote the well being of the weak. Once again, we note that the power which is necessary to promote justice can equally be used to promote injustice. This is precisely what has gone wrong with totalitarianism régimes that have set out to promote the interests of their own group within society. It is *how* a socialist government uses its power that is important, not the fact that it has that power.

(c) The Liberal Ideal of Freedom

To complete our discussion of freedom we turn to the concept of 'freedom' espoused by economic liberals.[1] The starting point for the

[1] There is a line of thought running from Locke, through Mill to Nozick and Ayn Rand. (See Ayn Rand *Capitalism: The Unknown Ideal* (New American history, 1962)). Particular expositions in the context of economic freedom are those of Hayek,
[Footnote continued on p.41]

analysis is that 'freedom of the individual, or perhaps the family, is our ultimate goal in judging social arrangements'. Freedom is defined negatively as that condition in which the coercion of some individuals by others is reduced to the minimum possible degree. The nature of freedom is independence of the arbitrary will of another, lack of interference, and lack of coercion. The starting point is again Locke's 'state of nature' where individuals are in a 'state of perfect freedom to order their actions and dispose of their persons and possessions as they think fit, within the bounds of the law of nature, without asking leave or dependency upon the will of any other man'. In the section on the state, we saw how Locke and Nozick then proceeded to justify the existence of a minimal state mainly to punish infraction of those individual liberties by others. We objected that this was scarcely compatible with the Christian teaching concerning the authorities in society. Here we explore the question as to whether the liberal concept of freedom as an overriding social objective is compatible with biblical criteria.

Before we do that, we need to expand the arguments of economic liberals that freedom is all of a piece, so that freedom is predicated on the existence of a free market economy. First, we notice that liberals accept a hierarchy of freedoms in those cases where these conflict. Moral and intellectual freedom are ranked highest, followed by political freedom. The economic freedoms of markets, competition, entry, choice of consumption and occupation, rank higher than 'freedoms' of contract and coalition. Second, it is argued, especially by Friedman, that the different types of freedom are intimately connected. The separation of economic freedom and individual freedom (e.g. in democratic socialism) is a delusion. The basic reason is that only in a market economy can the individual obtain resources to achieve his own ends and purposes without being dependent on others, apart from contracts freely entered into by both parties. The only prerequisites for such a system are the existence of 'law and order' to prevent coercion, and to enforce contracts. In such a system, what an individual does is strictly a private affair.

Our critique of this position is simply that the choice of individual freedom as defined by the liberals as the overriding value in assessing social arrangements, is incompatible with biblical criteria. That some element of freedom is a positive good is not denied. But it needs to be taken in conjunction with an equal emphasis on man in society with right, and obligations. Indeed, the biblical doctrine of fallen man should make us suspicious of any promotion of individual self-seeking as an ultimate value. Finally, we may well note that Friedman's association of freedom with market freedoms is open to objection. The outcome may well be freedom for the strong, and a greatly restricted range of options for the weak. But that is not a subject to be pursued here.[1]

---

[1] See D. A. Hay *A Christian Critique of Capitalism* (Grove Booklet on Ethics no. 5 (now 5a) 1975).

Footnote continued from page 40]
   Friedman, and Peacock and Rowley. (See C. K. Rowley and A. T. Peacock *Welfare Economics: A Liberal Restatement* (Martin Robertson, London, 1975)).

8. WORK

(a) The Biblical Doctrine of Work

Man's dignity and greatness stem from his creation in the image of God. His tragedy is the fall, which has marred the image, but not destroyed the purpose for which he was created. The contrast between the biblical anthropology, and the humanistic conception of man in economic analysis is nowhere more clearly shown than in the values given to work. Economic analysis sees work as a necessary evil in order to obtain purchasing power over goods and services. Marx described the worker's role as that of a wage slave. The biblical viewpoint is quite different.[1] First man has an obligation and a right to work. This is a creation provision, not a result of the fall. God, in whose image man is created, is described as a worker (Genesis 2.3) *before* the fall; man is created to subdue the earth and replenish it. He is placed in the garden of Eden to till it and to keep it. The Wisdom literature contains many exhortations to honest labour. Second, work should be meaningful and purposeful. This may be deduced from man's creation in the image of God, and the dominion that is assigned to him. Man's first activity, that of naming the animals, was a purposeful activity. But man is never encouraged to think of himself as 'creative' in the sense God is. His work is to explore, understand, and use, that which is given him by God in the created order. Man's creativity is no more than thinking God's thoughts after him, and humbly using the materials he has provided. The consequences of the fall for man's work are specifically described in Genesis 3.17-19. Work becomes toil and is subject to a curse. But that is the result of sin, and not God's intention. Work remains essential to human dignity, and integral to man's nature. Finally, the biblical view is that work is a social activity. Men should live together in communities and should share in work, each contributing his own particular skills. Each one has his own gifts to contribute: all share in the trusteeship over the created order. Once again the creation order has been sadly affected by the fall. No longer in right relationship with God, man finds it difficult to live in right relationship with his fellow men. The result is conflict, not least in the orgazisation of work. However, as Christians we will not accept this situation as God's intention for man.

This analysis of the biblical teaching concerning work needs to be related to the concept of stewardship. In Genesis 1 and 2 man the worker is given the stewardship of the created order. In the parable of the talents (Luke 19.11-27) each steward is given an initial endowment to work with. The basic point is that man cannot work without resources. The exhortations to work only have force when a man has access to the means of production.

This point can be illustrated from the law concerning the land. The account in Joshua 13-19 shows that each family was to be provided with a piece of land, which was to be held by that family in perpetuity. It should not be sold. It could be rented, but only until the Jubilee. The normal pattern of work was labour on the family land. Wage labour was

[1] A. Richardson *The Biblical Doctrine of Work* (S.C.M., London, 1973).

regarded as a form of social insurance (Deuteronomy 24.15) for those who had lost possession of their land until the next Jubilee. The prohibition of interest effectively implied that savings should be applied on the family land. Decisions about the use of the land were to be kept within the family. The returns were earnings representing the labour and initiative of the family, rather than profits. Large accumulations of wealth were avoided by provision for inheritance by all the sons, rather than primogeniture. Clearly some aspects of the law concerning the land relate specifically to the functioning of an agrarian economy (e.g. the injunctions concerning the moving of boundary markers). But there are also some general principles. First, it is clear that work and the stewardship of resources are linked. Man cannot operate without resources: he must have access to land, capital (tools or machinery) and training in the skills required. Second, stewards should control production rather than be dominated or merely 'hired' by capital. This is not only a precondition for the exercise of responsible stewardship: it should also provide incentives by ensuring that those who work share in the prosperity (or lack of prosperity) of the enterprise. Third, work involves co-operation not only with resources, but with other men. A division of labour in which each person contributes his own particular skills is no bad thing, so long as each can see his own contribution to the whole.

(b) Work in a Socialist System

There is little doubt that various socialist ideals concerning work closely mirror these Christian precepts. For example, the socialist ideal for work is that it should be a good to be enjoyed by every person according to his ability, and divorced from the need to earn a living. The alienation arising from the divorce of capital and labour, and the concept of competition, is to be replaced in socialism by an ideal of co-operation. In particular, the objectives of work should be controlled by the workers themselves, or at least determined in their interests, rather than by the bourgeoisie or other elite class pursuing their own interests. However it is open to discussion whether these ideals are in practice attained more fully in socialist than in capitalist systems.

Such evidence as there is of centrally planned communist economies suggest that they have been reasonably effective at maintaining high levels of employment for their people. Individual freedom of choice of occupation and of place of work is now followed in all European socialist countries, though membership of the Communist Party implies willingness to be directed. Communist governments have however resorted to direction of labour during periods of crisis, for example in China during the Cultural Revolution, when city dwellers and students were sent to work in the countryside. In theory the weapon of unemployment to ensure discipline is replaced by a disciplinary code administered by the trades unions, as a tool of the communist party. However the hope that socialist production would reduce alienation and induce a new attitude to work has proved singularly disappointing. The reason is that alienation of workers in capitalism is matched by an equal alienation in the 'state capitalism' of most centrally planned economies, and of nationalized industries in social democratic systems. The alienation arises partly from a divorce between the workers and the professional management, and partly from a sense that enterprise itself is directed by a bureaucratic planning authority. In planned economies the response has been an increasing reliance on material incentives, perhaps linked to enterprise performance, where the socialist ideal would be reliance on the moral incentive of working for the common good.

The basic defect of such a system, as with large firms in a capitalist system, is that it does not provide conditions under which workers can operate as responsible stewards. They need to be able to participate in decision making on issues concerning their work and future livelihood. The Yugoslav experiment in worker's management merits careful consideration in this respect. The operation of such firms has been described by Vanek.[1] The enterprise is formed and owned by a group of workers. A workers council within the firm recruits managers and key personnel, and approves the enterprise plan. This plan specifies the distribution of the firm's income between personal incomes, welfare (social consumption), capital and reserves. Personal remuneration is based on rules which are determined in advance, the actual values being determined by the success or otherwise of the enterprise. On the basis of his study, Vanek reached the following conclusions about the actual behaviour of such enterprises. The short run behaviour of the firm is directed to cost cutting, with prices based on costs. Profit maximization is seldom an objective. Survival and/or growth of the enterprise are the main long run objectives, and are the particular concern of the annual plans. Adjustment to changed business conditions, and the search for growing markets are the major content of such plans. There is an emphasis on accumulation of assets which are related to the welfare of the enterprise, not just for production, but for collective consumption.

Management is very important within such firms, in the provision of enterprise and initiative. Successful management is not frustrated by the worker's council. The trend is to workers' involvement by representation on the council, rather than general referenda of meetings of workers, especially in large firms. Income differentials within such firms seldom exceed the ratio 3:1, though differences *between* enterprises can be as large as 7:1, since they depend on the success of the enterprise. The enterprises have proved particularly well suited to expanding markets, but firms with declining markets have been reluctant to release workers (they cannot, of course, be dismissed). The lack of an active labour market makes it particularly difficult to transfer resources.

There is a substantial technical literature in economics which suggests that the Yugoslav system is inefficient in the allocation of resources. However, Vanek rejects this conclusion, on the grounds that the objectives assumed in such models cannot capture the reality of the Yugoslav firms. We would note that the concept of 'efficiency' used to arrive at such a conclusion is not necessarily compatible with a Christian assessment.

[1] J. Vanek *The Economics of Worker's Management* (George Allen and Unwin, London 1972).

A degree of worker participation in the management of firms has also formed part of the programmes espoused by the neo-Marxists, and by some social democrats. It was given added impetus by the publication of the Bullock Report. There is however a subtle difference of emphasis between the worker's *control* espoused by neo-Marxists for the operations of state enterprises (to match worker involvement in the planning process), and the less radical concept of worker participation or 'industrial democracy' of social democrats, including the Bullock Report.[1] Evidence on worker participation has been summarized by Wall and Lischeron.[2] They look at three aspects: the demand for participation, the effect of partipation on worker satisfaction, and employee response to worker participation schemes. It emerges that there is strong desire among workers for participation in decisions affecting the immediate work environment of the individual. The evidence is scanty on desire for 'distant' participation: generally there is no demand for worker control though some involvement in higher decision taking would be welcome. A difficulty with this evidence is that workers may have very little idea as to what distant participation would involve, and find it difficult to express views on the subject. Wall and Lischeron are cautious about accepting the conclusions of empirical studies that participation in immediate decisions has improved worker satisfaction. For example studies that depend on turnover rates and absenteeism are not measuring satisfaction *per se,* and such indicators can reflect other factors in the situation which are difficult to control for in the analysis. The same is true for experimental studies which show higher productivity. On more distant participation, the evidence from Israel and West Germany, is unambiguous that employee response to the opportunity for influencing company policy has been minimal. There are two reasons for this. The schemes have been imposed by legislation and are not always well suited to the conditions of a particular enterprise. Worker directors have proved to be ineffectual, and this has been perceived by the workers themselves.

Three broad conclusions are stressed. First, that workers prefer a system in which the responsibility of control is shared by workers and managers rather than worker control *per se.* Within that system, control should be biased towards workers at the local or immediate level and towards managers at the strategic level. Second, worker participation should be direct, and not via an intermediary body such as a trade union. Third, that participation must be taken in conjunction with other variables such as the degree of trust and openness between the personalities involved in decisions, the problem solving strategies adopted, the means of resolving role conflicts and the communications within the enterprise. A formal participation scheme without progress in these other areas may increase worker frustration and alienation, not reduce it.

[1] Department of Trade (UK) *Report of the Committee of Inquiry on Industrial Democracy* (The Bullock Report) Cmnd 6706, 1977 (HMSO).

[2] T. D. Wall and J. A. Lischeron *Worker Participation* (McGraw-Hill (UK), London, 1977).

9. ECONOMIC EQUALITY

The existence of material inequality has been a pivot in the moral criticism of capitalism in socialist writings, and the search for more equality has been a part of the ideals pursued by socialist programmes. So we need to consider equality as an ideal from the standpoint of the biblical doctrine of man.

(a) Biblical teaching on the rich and the poor

In one respect the Bible does treat men as equal, and that is in relation to God. In God's sight all men are equal in their fallenness, and in their need for salvation. In that very fundamental sense all men *are* equal. However that does not help us very much in the consideration of social and economic equality. We may recall from the previous section our conclusion that every man should work, and should have access to resources so that his work may be fruitful. There can be little doubt that fulfilment of that condition would eliminate much of the inequality that exists in our world. However, the biblical material goes further. A person may have great resources at his disposal: personal abilities, property and technical information. He has the obligation to use those resources fruitfully, as a steward. But *consumption* of the proceeds is subject to other Biblical teaching. First, the presumption is that every person has the right to share in God's provision for mankind. The creation was for man in general. For the maintenance of human dignity every person needs a minimum standard in food, clothing and shelter. God provided food and clothing for Adam and Eve (Genesis 3.21). In the Law, the poor and landless are given a share in the harvest. A man who has pawned his coat should be allowed to have it back for the night to sleep in. In the Sermon on the Mount, Jesus explicitly refers to food and clothing as God's provision for man (Matthew 6.25-32). Paul enjoins Timothy to be content with food and clothing (1 Timothy 6.8).

By contrast with the minimum described, biblical teaching also suggests that there is a maximum standard to which a man should attain. The matter has been well analysed by J. V. Taylor[1], setting out the biblical teaching on greed and covetousness. The prophetic condemnation of greed and luxury in Amos 6 is paralleled by James 5.1-5 in the New Testament, with a warning of God's impending judgment on the rich. The point is that when the rich fail in their obligation to the poor, then God's judgment follows (Isaiah 10.1-4, Matthew 25.31-46). As the Magnificat suggests, God is very jealous in his defence of the poor. The seriousness with which God views covetousness is indicated by its prohibition in the Ten Commandments. Jesus puts it into a list of evils on a par with adultery and murder (Mark 7.22).

(b) Equality in Socialist Thought and Practice

There is no doubt that a number of these biblical themes find a precise parallel in socialist ideals. Indeed the Judaeo-Christian intellectual inheritance is almost certainly the source of these ideals. Thus socialists have emphasized the need to eradicate absolute poverty, in

[1] J. V. Taylor *Enough is Enough* (S.C.M., London, 1975).

which men do not have the minimum conditions for human existence. They have drawn attention to the need for each person to have adequate conditions for exercising their abilities, stressing the need for equal opportunity. They have denied that those who have great resources at their disposal also have the right to consume the proceeds of those resources, regardless of the condition of their fellow men. They have extolled the ideal of a classless society as 'one in which men will be separated from each other less sharply by variations in wealth and origin, than by differences in character'.[1] The biblical assertions that a man's life does not consist in the abundance of his possessions is mirrored by Marx's criticism of commodity fetishism, and his dream of a society where goods will be so abundant that man will no longer be dominated by the need to produce. He will be creative rather than hedonistic.

It remains to be seen whether socialist programmes have been a means to achieve these ideals. There have been three main elements in socialist programmes. The first is the reduction, or abolition, of property incomes. In communist societies with all the means of production socially owned, the surplus after paying the workers returns to the state (or planning board) to be re-invested or to be used in socialized consumption (welfare programmes etc.). Depending on the degree of centralization in the planning process, this allocation may be determined centrally or even at the firm level (in the Yugoslav system). In socialist societies, where an extensive privately-owned sector still exists, despite nationalization of major sectors and firms, the aim has been to restrict the accumulation of large wealth holdings by taxes on capital and especially on inheritance. Now there is nothing in biblical teaching that requires us to deny to individuals the stewardship of great resources, so long as they exercise that stewardship fruitfully and unselfishly. Thus a socialist programme aimed at property in itself cannot be justified without either the presumption that large accumulations of wealth will not be wisely administered, or that the power which they give to individuals will be used to protect their (selfish) interests against any state which sought to promote justice (e.g. by redistributive taxation of property incomes). However the biblical ideal of providing each person with resources to work with, so that he can exercise stewardship, also needs to be taken into account here, in the consideration of equal opportunity.

The idea of equal opportunity is that each individual should have equal chances of developing his own abilities, and that access to all positions of responsibility should be based on capacity to undertake the tasks. Questions of class or family background, or of family wealth, should not enter in determining a person's education of work responsibilities. The means of achieving these objectives are mainly via the educational system. A positive step is the provision of education as a public good; more radical measures include the banning of private education, by means of which the rich can obtain specially privileged facilities for their offspring. In addition, appointments to positions of

---

[1] R. Jenkins 'Equality' in R. H. S. Crossman (ed.) *New Fabian Essays* (2nd ed. London, 1970).

responsibility are to be made on the basis of open competitions with the selection criteria made public. A further step would be 'positive discrimination' in appointments in favour of applicants from backgrounds where they have had difficulty in developing their talents. Within the framework of equal opportunity it is admitted that differential rewards may remain great, given that individuals have very different gifts. The difficulty with all this, as Crosland[1] shrewdly observed, is that it results in the creation of a meritocratic élite which is just as keen to protect its own class interests as the capitalists and property owners. It was this 'new class' that Milovan Djilas castigated in the development of communist societies. It is easier to define the ideal, than the type of social arrangements that will give rise to it.

The third element in socialist programmes under this head is the emphasis on social consumption goods. Depending on the particular socialist régime a wide range of goods and services are provided free, on the basis of need, rather than by purchase. Examples are medical care, education, legal advice, housing, public transport and recreation and entertainment. The idea is to give access to certain minimum facilities on an equal basis to each member of the society. When linked with cash benefits (e.g. to families, unemployed persons, the retired and the chronically sick) these form a very major step to the provision of a minimum standard of life for all citizens. There is no doubt that this is in line with the biblical provisions in the Law for the poor and disadvantaged (in a much less complex society, of course, than most modern societies). Naturally these goods and services have to be paid for, and the source varies from diversion of enterprise surpluses (in communist countries) to taxes on income and profits in socialist mixed economies. Programmes of this kind are always subject to a risk of waste, and of fraudulent claims in respect of financial benefits. However the existence of such difficulties should not surprise a Christian. But they cannot be put forward as a reason for abandoning such programmes, given reasonable safeguards in administration. The needs of the many should not be ignored because of the dishonesty of the few.

Finally, we should stress again that the biblical criteria in this area are addressed to the question of redressing inequality, especially poverty. There is no concept of economic equality as an objective. A particular stress is on giving each person access to resources so that he can exercise his stewardship, and provide for himself. The provision of a 'safety net' to maintain each person at a minimum level is secondary within this system. For example, the primary emphasis in the Law is on every family having access to land. The provisions for wage labour, and for the poor to share in the harvest are secondary. This means that a Christian will find more to support in programmes that provide employment and access to resources, than in those that are seeking economic equality in consumption by redistributive taxation and transfer payments, essential though these may be as a safety net.

[1] C. A. R. Crosland *The Future of Socialism* (Jonathan Cape, London, 1956).